Dog & Puppy Matters

SARA WHITTAKER

First Edition

First printed in the United Kingdom

Published by Whittaker Publishing

Paperback ISBN-13: 978-1-9168726-0-8
Paperback ISBN-13: 978-1-9168726-1-5

Whittaker Publishing
5 Harold Street
Leicester LE2 8AL

Dog
& Puppy Matters

SARA WHITTAKER

CONTENTS

INTRODUCTION

Dogs have always played a large part in my life. As a child, I grew up with dogs that were treated as part of the family. Holidays and days out were always planned with the dogs in mind. They were rarely left for long and never saw the inside of a boarding kennel. They slept with us, choosing which bed they fancied each night, and liked nothing better than to curl up on the sofa, either with each other or with one of us. I cannot remember any occasion where the dogs caused any of us undue concern – except for one of our Boston terriers who regularly humped a cushion when he was young, causing my Mum to be inundated with embarrassing questions from my brother and me!

My parents bought me a Jack Russell terrier, that I called Rocky, when I was a teenager. Determined to be a good dog owner I researched how he should be trained and looked after. I was more than a little surprised to discover that the way we lived with our pets was, according to the book, totally wrong – we were treating them as family, kids even, and not dogs at all. Armed with this new info I embarked on a soul-destroying mission to ensure my Jack Russell did not become 'top dog' over us, much to the amusement of my father.

Instead of having a loving and rewarding bond with my dog, I ended up with many problems and a relationship based on confrontation and denial. It took me many years to admit that the books I read were wrong and that my father (and my gut instinct) were right! Having finally jumped over this hurdle, I began once again to enjoy the relationship with my pets that I had as a child. This was a big turning point for me, and has been for many of my clients over the years. To finally have the freedom to live and behave as our instinct dictates, rather than leading a rather false existence with those close to us.

Dog & Puppy Matters... is aimed at sharing my experiences, thoughts and beliefs on how we can live happily with our dogs. Understanding an animal's feelings and emotions is no different to accepting that the many people we live and share our lives with sometimes have difficulties and need our help and guidance. Through my pet behaviour practice WitsEnd® I have been able, over many years, to help hundreds of people who've had problems with their dogs. The dog training school, originally set up in the vegetable patch in my back garden and now run in a purpose-designed facility, has seen over 10,000 dogs pass through the door.

My general philosophy of living with – *not against* – dogs has been broadly accepted with open arms (and not a little relief) by those who share my love and fascination for these incredible creatures!

SARA WHITTAKER

Sara Whittaker works from her Leicester-based business, WitsEnd®, where she currently runs training classes for dogs of all ages and abilities. She also practices behaviour therapy for dogs and cats with problems ranging from aggression to separation related disorders.

In addition, Sara was an external lecturer at The College of Animal Welfare. She taught students, the general public, pet professionals and veterinary professionals on a range of subjects including dog and cat behaviour issues, setting up puppy parties or classes, aggression problems and dealing with common behaviour matters.

Dog & Puppy Matters… is a revised and updated version of *Think Pet!*, which was published in February 2005.

Sara has two grown up children and currently four dogs: a black pug named Strumpet who is a stinky food addict, Parsnip the needy springer, Cricket the gorgeous (and knows it sproodle and Pancake the crazy cockapoo.

CHAPTER ONE

You Know More Than You Think

1.1 You Know Your Dog

Trust your instincts. You know your dog and I'll bet you know more than you think about keeping dogs. Deep down, *you* know *your* dog well. You can read his mood, ascertain what he wants, and fulfil his needs like no one else. As a dog owner you know when he is unhappy or stressed. But we don't trust ourselves. We turn to friends, textbooks, books like this and professionals for advice, instead of relying on our own instincts, which are often right!

As a species, we humans are designed to nurture. We are one of the few species that looks after its young long after they can look after themselves. This instinctual need to nurture is a part of us and makes us what we are. We are not born with an instruction manual complete with troubleshooting guide, but we usually want to do our best. Our instinct to look after something is why we have dogs and pets generally.

1.2 You Are Not Alone

Our dogs are a different species to us, so of course you have many questions about them. You might think your concerns regarding your dog are unique, and in many ways they are, as your dog is an individual with its own distinctive personality. However, dog owners throughout the world have the same queries, (some minor, some vast), and we all experience 'situations' from time to time that we feel we can't cope with on our own.

1.3 Relationships

Living with others in harmony is all about two-way communication. Relationships have to be worked at, from both sides, irrespective of who is involved. From partner to children, parents to friends, every association we have requires some sort of input from us on a regular basis. Our dogs are no different. They require understanding and empathy through difficult periods. They need things that uplift them and make them feel good. They depend on us for food, water, and help with general healthcare, but above all else they want love and affection.

The relationship between an owner and dog is strong. The nurturing bond is about as robust as you can get. Having someone depend on you feeds the need to look after him or her, and looking after him or her feeds the dependence. But we have been conditioned to feel a bit guilty about having a special relationship with our dogs. Many clients have said, in countless behaviour consultations, that they allow their dog onto the settee or that it sleeps in the bed with them. 'I know it's wrong,' they whisper guiltily. What is surely wrong is for people to feel bad about something that is so good. Your relationship with your dog is very personal, as is mine. We share our homes and our lives with them. And how we choose to live with them is an individual decision.

Dogs are very special.

1.4 Dominating Your Dog

Do we need to dominate our dogs? Do we need to dominate anything or anyone that lives with us? In my opinion the answer is no. Why invite a dog or puppy to live with you, and then try and control his every move? What we need is a strong relationship, built on good communication, trust and love. We have to understand our dogs' needs and try to fulfil them. We can teach him with clear, consistent signals how we want him to behave in differing situations. By sticking to simple ground rules, we can educate our dogs to do what is expected of them quickly and without confusion.

1.5 Dogs Dominating Us

Do our dogs need to dominate us? In my view the answer is again no. Dominance is controlling behaviour. When a dog is labelled as 'dominant' it means he either believes he controls, or is trying to control, the family, house and garden – aiming for the status of 'top dog'. This makes him sound more like a terrorist, planning a coup in the house!

Dogs are naturally opportunistic: they will take every opportunity to bring themselves pleasure. This can sometimes make them appear manipulative and self-centred, but hey! It is the nature of the beast.

Some experts suggest we impose rigorous conditions on dogs to avoid them controlling us and to ensure we control them. Strict rules are designed to 'take the dog down a peg or two', and include such things as removing all their toys, feeding them after we have eaten, sitting in their beds to show them who's boss, and ignoring them when they seek our attention. What we really have to ask is, what do these rules mean to our dog, and how much of this approach is really necessary? (See 1.7.)

Excessive discipline directly affects our dogs' general happiness. Their emotions will vary from mild insecurity because their owners aren't taking any notice of them, to heightened anxiety because the rules are simply too much for the animal to cope with. They might feel intense frustration at having all their pleasures removed. Imagine how you would feel if you no longer had access to things, people, or activities you enjoyed: you'd be depressed, angry, frustrated, miserable, and stressed!

In some households, changes in the dog's emotional state could be deemed a success – for instance the very lively, over-bearing attention-seeker suddenly becomes sullen and quiet when all his pleasures are taken away. The questions we have to ask ourselves are:

- Is this really a long-term effect, or will he eventually seek rewards in other ways?
- Has he learned to behave differently, or is he simply feeling differently about his circumstances?
- Is this really a success for the animal?
- *Do I really want to live with my dog like this???*

Many dogs, especially those that cause problems for their owners, are too easily labelled as dominant. I have had cases referred to me as dominance problems, when in fact the animals were frightened, nervous, hyperactive – anything but controlling. Their emotional response was perhaps linked to previous learning or a current situation. When a behaviour pattern is explained in terms of the dog's emotional behaviour – how he thinks and feels – often the dog's 'parent' can find his or her own answer to the problem. Through proper understanding a solution often shines through.

Our dogs do try to manipulate us, not because they are born 'control freaks', but because they are essentially selfish in nature and want what is rewarding to them. We need to firstly accept this, and then look closely at how we deal with it.

1.6 What Can Happen

It is important to consider what the dominance theory can do to the nurturing relationship, the emotional bond that develops between dog and owner. If the owner has removed most of the reasons for having the dog in the first place – something to look after, companionship, shared experiences, and mutual affection – the dog may no longer trust his owner and perhaps view him with suspicion. The majority of dog owners I have met are uncomfortable with the dominance concept, but they may not have been offered an alternative view.

Sheba was a two-year-old German shepherd female referred to me for 'dominant-aggressive' problems towards her owners. But she was only aggressive to 'Mum and Dad': with their two-year-old son, Jack, Sheba was a perfect angel. She was calm around him, never murmured when he pulled her hair or tweaked her ears, and even acted as his walking aid when he took his first steps. She had never bitten, choosing rather to growl menacingly at her owners in specific situations, like when they sent her to her bed or tried to get her to do anything such as sit. Sheba would allow Jack to play mischievously with her food, but if his parents so much as looked in her direction when she was eating she would grumble.

Having taken professional advice, Sheba's owners were told she was dominant (which they already knew as they had read all the books), and was trying to rule the house. They were advised she needed to be brought back into line. Certain strict rules were to be instigated immediately, such as taking all Sheba's toys away and only allowing her to have them when her owners said so. Sheba was not to be fed until her owners had eaten. Her access around the property was to be restricted to the kitchen and garden only, and she was not to have contact with Jack as she was 'too dangerous'. Sheba was put on a choke chain when walking and was schooled to obey instantly every command given, by force if necessary.

Sheba became more aggressive within a few days of these changes. One of the reasons she got worse was not having contact with Jack, the one person in the house who didn't threaten her. Instead he played with her and gave her love, affection and pleasure. Sheba was aggressive to her 'Mum and Dad' because most of her interaction with them had been negative – shouting, forcing her into her bed and removing her food. She simply felt threatened by her owners, who incidentally loved her dearly. What a mess!

Her owners felt terribly let down. They had, after all, followed all the rules from day one of owning Sheba as a young puppy. They'd read all the books and had trainers out to the house, as well as taking her to classes. They had come to the conclusion that she had been born bad and nothing would change her. It took just a bit of explaining how Sheba was feeling - threatened and insecure, with no real pleasure in her life – for the penny to drop. Once they understood the basic principle that 'dogs have feelings too,' we began to make alterations to their daily lives to ensure Sheba had regular 'fixes of pleasure' – games, toys, training using food treats (see 4.21 to 4.30) and of course contact with her beloved Jack. Simply fitting a head collar to Sheba made it possible for her 'Mum' to take her to the park every day with Jack in his buggy, something she had previously not been able to do, as Sheba pulled and choked herself on her chain.

Training Sheba to go to her bed willingly was easy. We just had to motivate her to want to do it, or rather to do it happily and not feel punished by it. Putting a special toy stuffed with treats in her bed did the trick, changing her perception of the bed from punitive to rewarding. The food aggression problem was side-stepped by throwing out the food bowl that she had been 'taught' to guard and replacing it with a food cube that she could roll around and feed herself from (see 4.22). But the biggest difference came from the owners' change in attitude. Released from the rigid regime of always ensuring Sheba didn't become 'top dog', they felt free and able to communicate with her as a valued and much loved member of the family.

1.7 Commonly Used Techniques I Wouldn't Recommend

I've worked with dogs with behavioural issues for many, many years and still have yet to meet a dominant dog. I'm going to list the methods here that are commonly used to reduce a dogs 'status' – with my take on what the dog might think is happening.

a. You must walk in front of your dog or he will think he is leading the pack to go hunting.

This assumes that the pack leader is always the fastest chaser in the hunt, however the pack leader in most social groups is typically the best communicator. And taking your dog for a walk in most cases is not a hunting situation! Dogs pull on the lead because they want to get to where they are going faster; it then becomes a habit – simple.

b. Ignore your dog if he approaches for attention.

This is designed to make the dog feel insecure and not get pushy, but in reality it can start to undermine your relationship as the dog may feel you are unapproachable. However, it does depend on the method employed to get your attention! Avid attention seekers will employ a myriad of approaches to get your attention and these should be ignored. Likewise ignoring your dog while he is resting is not a punishment – its just common sense.
Trust is hard earned and easily lost and this is one way

to go about eroding it. Some dogs could feel punished or that they are in trouble and become anxious. Ignoring any social creature is quite a severe punishment, as you will no doubt understand if you have ever been 'sent to Coventry'.

c. Ignore your dog when you get home.

Ignoring your dog's attentions when you get home will probably make him try harder (jump harder, nip at clothing etc.) to get your attention (see 5.11). Some dogs will feel upset (as in point b), which could start separation type problems – toileting or chewing when left because the manner of the owner, when returning home, upsets the dog. I can't think of anything worse than getting home and my dog not even getting out of his bed to greet me. There's something a little unnatural about this rule. Obviously you don't want the dog going mad so you need to keep everything low key.

d. Take all the dog's toys away and only let him have one when you say – so you control them.

Dogs like to play with toys and if there are none they will play with whatever is available; a mobile phone, slippers or a nice stuffed cushion. Those canines who are not into toys simply won't notice what you have done except that the house is tidier!

e. Feed the dog after you have eaten.

This is another one of the 'wolf pack' theories. The leader always eats first – but does he? If a dog eats immediately after you (which is the only way he is going to know something's up – see 4.9) then he may start drooling in anticipation. This is not something a dog has any control over, so he's not being naughty. He may also start staring at your plate because the sight of you eating will remind him that he will be fed soon, making him even hungrier than usual. I always feed the dogs first, then they are happy and digesting their meal while I relax and eat mine.

f. Don't play tug-of-war as it allows the dog to pit his strength against you.

Tuggy is a great game to play and many dogs really enjoy it. There are a few dogs out there that get hyper excitable with this game and it's not really for them. The rest love it and there is no sensible reason not to play. Dogs do growl when they are playing – especially this game. Your dog isn't growling at you and it will not teach him to be aggressive.

g. If you do play tug of war then the human must win the toy.

This is quite an amusing rule. Dogs don't really understand the concept of winning and if you do let go while playing, the dog may toss the toy around for a few seconds and then fetch it back to you, possibly rubbing it against your hand or leg to encourage you to play again. It's the game a dog enjoys, the interaction – not winning as this means the game is effectively over.

h. Keep the dog off the furniture.

There is no earthly reason why a dog cannot go on the settee, except that you may want to sit there and he is possibly big and muddy. This is a personal choice so don't feel guilty about cuddling up to your dog on the sofa. There is a small scattering of dogs that become selfish over the settee and can get grumpy. No different to the dog that growls when it has a butcher's bone. We would obviously say 'no' to bones for that dog and never give them. Equally we should not let the grumpy dog guard the settee from us – so those dogs shouldn't be allowed up. I stress it is only a small number of dogs that do this – you hear about them because they make entertaining TV and magazine articles. Just remember though, a dog doesn't know he's filthy so make your choice wisely. Many people put a dog blanket on the sofa and the dog is allowed up only when that is present – they learn this very quickly.

i. Don't allow the dog upstairs.

Why? Again this comes down to personal choice so don't feel guilty about having the dog in the bedroom – or the bed! Your relationship with your dog is unique to you. And if it causes you no problems then there is no reason why not. (Vacuuming the bed is optional.)

j. Confine the dog so he does not have free access into the living room.

This is about separating the dog from the family group so he's not part of the household. The aim is to make the dog more biddable and remove confidence by making him feel insecure and an 'outsider'. It kind of takes away the point of having a dog really. They like to be with us – they are social animals that love company. It is important not to allow young puppies the run of the house until house trained, or you may come across deposits that are several days old secreted under beds and behind laundry baskets! That's just common sense. You have to keep your eye on a puppy.

k. Don't allow a dog to lie in doorways as he is controlling the house.

You have to ask the question why a dog would want to lie in a doorway. These places tend to be cooler, so for the dog that feels the central heating it might be more comfortable. Some breeds herd and some are just plain nosey. As part of the herding instinct comes an innate awareness of where your group is. A doorway is a good place to mentally 'herd' the flock. The nosey dog (of which there are too many to mention) might find the doorway a useful place to be just in case, ensuring he never misses anything that might be beneficial. The opportunist nature is never far away in even the most devoted of dogs.

l. Take ownership of the dog's bed by sitting in it.

Possibly the funniest rule – and what's even more amusing is that people actually do it. And what is going through the dog's head at that time, I wonder? 'OK, you sit there. I'll take the sofa!' It would appear from my enquiries that many dogs try and get in with their owner, or sit back head tilted, looking perplexed. It would seem that they just don't get it.

m. Remove the puppy or dog's food while he's eating, to ensure you can.

It has to be said this is the quickest way to teach a dog to guard its food. Many dogs will accept food removal without a problem, but some will tense up, start growling and defend the food. And you have just achieved what you were trying to avoid. Better to add food to the bowl or just swirl your hand around in it for a second – handling the food but not threatening to remove it. Once the puppy is relaxed with this you could take the bowl away and add more food – teaching the same thing in a less confrontational manner.

These rules were designed many years ago to create a dog who 'knows his place', but there seems little point in owning a dog if this is how you have to live with it and having a hamster in a cage might be a better option.

1.8 What Dogs Mean to Us

Our dogs are our friends. They are an outlet for our affections and give us something to love and look after, regardless of what else is going on in our lives. When no one else loves us, there is always our furry friend to rely on. We can tell them our innermost secrets, knowing they will never be revealed. We don't have to dress to impress our dogs. They don't look at us first thing in the morning and criticise our puffy eyes, pale cheeks or lank hair.

When I was a wild youngster and living on my own, having my dog gave me stability and made me responsible. He was a good reason to go home. Stroking an animal is calming and therapeutic. It even unwinds you, reducing heart rate and blood pressure!

1.9 What We Mean to our Dogs

The special 'parental' relationship we have with our dogs is the basis for their very existence. Dogs wouldn't exist in their current form if it weren't for our desire to look after them.

The evolution of the dog into a domestic animal happened many thousands of years ago. Proven by DNA to have evolved from the wolf, the dog still retains many wolf-like characteristics – interestingly, only those of the juvenile wolf. It would appear the nurturing bond with us arrested the 'new wolf's' development at the juvenile stage, ensuring it never quite grew up.

Wolves once scavenged from the waste disposal dumps on the outskirts of our ancestors' settlements. Some of these wolves were less afraid of people and produced young with the same tolerance. Growing up in the presence of people, their confidence with people increased. The young wolves in particular began to bond with humans in a special way when they came into close contact. Man began to feed and nurture these young wolves, creating the parent/child relationship and the dependency this brings. Man began to select the cubs, first for friendliness, and then to breed them for guarding and hunting. The wolves would also have protected the area from other roving wolf packs, driving all potential competition away and protecting the human inhabitants.

The nurturing relationship is as important to our dogs as it is to us. Our dogs need us more than anything else, though this does not mean they want our sole attention all the time. Other things such as hunting the neighbour's cat or sleeping on a nice sunspot on the settee will also matter to them.

1.10 Breeds

The dog has been bred for many different functions – hunting, herding, guarding – and one dog can look entirely different from another. Breed differences in the dog are vast and are mainly based upon their hunting sequence of eye, stalk, chase, pounce, bite, kill. The collie for example has been bred to repeatedly 'eye, stalk, chase', over and over again – obsessively in some cases. Terriers, on the other hand, are pre-wired to do the whole sequence very quickly and without deviation. Pointers just do 'eye', and look very stately at the same time. Breeding for differing functions over thousands of years has altered the dog's appearance dramatically.

Doing what you are designed to do makes you happy. Dogs are no exception to this. A dog feels blissful after a good sniff and run around in the woods or a fast chase game with a ball depending upon its breed function. But different breeds require different approaches to keep them happy.

Knowing this gives us plenty of options to keep our animals mentally and physically stimulated.

CHAPTER TWO

Useful Things to Know Early On

2.1 Teaching Names

Teaching your puppy its name is first in a long line of things they need to learn, and choosing the name is the first step. Two-syllable names are the easiest for our pets to grasp – for example Tosca, Mutley, Bailey and Maisie. Long names are nice but may need shortening for everyday use. For instance the English bull terrier called Mr Pink had his name shortened to Pinky – a bit of a comedown from *Reservoir Dogs* to *Pinky and Perky*! – but I don't suppose he cared.

Most puppies learn their names quickly without us really having to do any specific training for it. Just using it while paying the puppy attention is often enough. If not, try this. Call your pup's name in a cheerful and excited voice, while he is quite close to you. If he looks around, or comes to you, show you are happy by stroking him, giving him a food treat or offering a game of something he likes. Try not to over-use the name, as your pup may learn to ignore it. Only call him if you want him for something nice.

Being called, and then told off, is a very quick method of teaching your dog its name is not a pleasant thing to hear.

2.2 Feeding – What and How Often

There are many different pet foods on the market and no single brand of food suits all dogs. Very young puppies require feeding little and often. There growth rate is such that we have to 'reload' them every few hours so they have the nutrients to help them develop. Most puppies are on four meals per day when they move to their new homes at eight weeks. These are cut down over the weeks to two meals per day at approximately six to eight months and then kept on two meals per day for life. Years ago we would cut down further and feed them only one meal per day. Current thinking is to feed two meals, morning and evening, which aids digestion, prevents serious stomach disorders and keeps energy levels steady. It also stops our dogs from becoming grumpy because they are hungry and feeling low.

Puppy foods are formulated to give them what they need during their growing period. Once they have finished growing they can go onto an adult formula. There is no set time a puppy should go onto adult food, as the diets are all different and so are the breed sizes! Always read the packs to find out about your dog's diet.

Large breeds of dog may require feeding three smaller meals per day, as their growth rate can continue up to and beyond 18 months of age (most dogs are fully grown at a year). Specialist 'large breed' diets are now available. These are formulated to keep the growth rate steady and to increase the strength of bones and joints – potential problem areas for the very large dog. These diets are usually given for the first two years.

A good diet is one that provides a complete, balanced meal – and one that the animal will eat. There is little point in providing a 'top notch' dinner if the dog refuses to eat it. With the excellent range of good quality diets available there should be no problem in finding one that suits your individual pet. Some dogs will eat anything put in front of them, while others are more discerning. If your dog is being a fusspot, don't just think about what you are providing, but also how much you are giving and how you're presenting it (see 4.21 to 4.25 to learn how you can make food fun). Many dog food manufacturers rather overstate the amount needed and sometimes feeding a smaller amount solves the problem instantly (see 7.8).

Over-feeding can produce a 'fatty', as many dogs will literally eat until they burst. But there are dogs that will just walk away. You think they don't like the food, whereas in reality they are still full from the last meal.

Some dogs inhale food – even making them sick in the process. This does nothing for their table manners, let alone the poor digestive system, and can lead to tummy ache and wind! Use a 'slow-down' bowl or Green Feeder (a good pet store will have these). This is a bowl with lumpy or 'sticky outy' bits moulded into the bottom. The dog has to work around these lumps to get to his food. This type of bowl works very well. Alternatively you can use food-dispensing toys or scatter the food around the floor or garden to slow the puppy down (see 4.21 to 4.26).

2.3 How Much Rest Does a Puppy Need? – Grumpy and Manic Pups

For years all us behaviourists and trainers have been saying 'stimulate, stimulate, stimulate'. But there is such a thing as over-stimulating and that is something I have seen quite a lot of in the last few years. Think about a children's party full of lively young humans in their best party frocks, music, games, pass-the-parcel, a bouncy castle and lots of food to keep them energised. They all have a wonderful time and run from one activity to the other at break-neck pace. About twenty minutes from the end it all goes wrong. Martha has fallen and bumped her knee, something that she would normally shrug off but for some reason she is beside herself and screaming, red faced, for her Mum. Then Jason jumps a little too wildly in the castle and head-butts Peter who becomes irate and starts yelling whose fault it is and that not only had Jason ambushed him in the castle but he cheated at pass-the-parcel too. Are you getting the picture? Chaos ensues and all the kids go home to their respective families in a frazzled state clutching their party bags and grumping 'It's not fair' about everything and anything. This is an example of over-stimulation – human style.

Now we relate back to our furry friends and we can perhaps see that sometimes they get frazzled too. The classic example of this is the puppy that is great all day and then becomes a crazed, red-eyed monster in the evenings that won't – or more accurately *can't* – settle down. At this time the puppy can be running about the room nipping and yapping, dive-bombing anyone who dares sit down and stealing anything that will guarantee a reaction. Some even become aggressive and start growling and snarling.

Typical examples of this are puppies that have owners at home all day – each time the owner moves, the puppy moves – so he could effectively be on the go from dawn until dusk with no sleep. And sleep could be quite difficult if the pup's bed is in a busy area or he is of the type of character that won't settle easily. This is where a crate comes into its own (see 3.20). Settle the puppy in a quiet room, away from the hubbub, in his crate or doggy den. If needed cover the crate with a sheet, so all stimulation is effectively removed. Put on a radio, turned down low, to reduce the impact of noises from elsewhere and let him have a well-earned nap. Do this at least twice per day, after food and exercise in the morning and again in the afternoon. Some very lively pups need an extra nap after their evening meal. You'll have a different dog within a few days.

This crazy behaviour should not be confused with the wall of death behaviour that all puppies do. This involves arching the back, tucking the legs underneath and hightailing it around the room for a few minutes in an outpouring of energy. This is funny, great for the pup and completely normal.

I saw a nine-month-old springer spaniel recently. His name was Dave and he was a typical lively version of the breed. During the day he became increasingly more aggressive to his Mum, goading her to get attention by getting on the furniture and then growling at her when she tried to 'hoik' him off, stealing her sons' toys even though he had *loads* of toys himself. This behaviour persisted and got steadily worse from about 11am, right through until bedtime. Mum was being driven steadily crazy by Dave and all advice pointed towards increasing his exercise, playing more games with him and basically giving him more entertainment. But she had two children under the age of four who also needed attention. One day Dave bit her, so she booked him in for behaviour therapy. (He could quite easily have been put to sleep for this – it happens!)

All we did with Dave was to change his food to a hypoallergenic diet to make sure nothing in his food was fuelling his activities – just to be on the safe side. And put him in his crate for a sleep in the utility room three times per day. Within hours, Dave was a different dog.

The house was just too stimulating for Dave and he was of the type that if something was going on – he had to be a part of it. A nosey, curious dog, that didn't know when to call it a day and chill: instead of becoming lethargic and tired looking he became manic and just a little crazy. This is more common than you think and I have seen many cases and helped many people in puppy classes with this simple, but effective advice.

Indeed, in puppy classes this problem often becomes obvious in the last few minutes at the end of the hour when the pups are bombing around having a well-earned play. Some just become unmanageable and playtime, for them, has to be curtailed early.

2.4 How Much Should You Exercise?

If you think about a puppy's growth rate – it is very steep. They grow alarmingly quickly sometimes and it almost seems like inches are added each day. As the pup's body finishes growing the bones harden and the skeleton is finally formed. During this period of growth the dog is very susceptible to changes in its bone structure and long-term damage can be caused easily. Sometimes this is caused by poor nutrition, but mostly over-exercise is the culprit.

The general rule of thumb is five minutes for every month of life. So, a 16week old puppy should be walked roughly twenty minutes, up to three times per day as long as these walks are spread out and not all done at once. There is breed variance with this and if you are unsure then contact your veterinary practice for individual advice.

The twenty minutes should be a mixture of on and off-lead exercise – fifteen minutes on lead and five off would be a good ratio.

This exercise regime takes into consideration that the puppy will be moving about your house and garden on and off throughout the day so please don't crate your puppy for the rest of the time. A six-months-old Dogue de Bordeaux came to us for classes. This was a few years ago. It was so weak it could hardly stand. The puppy's owners had been advised by the breeder not to allow it to exercise – and they had taken this advice a little too literally. So the dog had developed no leg muscle to support its body weight. Hydrotherapy and controlled exercise had him up and about in no time, but only time will tell if there is any long-term damage.

2.5 Inoculations

Years ago our dogs carried, and died from, many diseases. These diseases are still killers and each time a dog contracts one of them, it is likely that others will become infected. Now, as with our children, we immunise our pets. The vaccines for dogs cover Parvovirus, Hepatitis, Leptospirosis, Distemper and Para-influenza.

These are the vaccinations that your puppy should receive before being allowed out in areas inhabited by other dogs. A routine booster vaccination each year continues the protection. The first vaccinations are given at set ages, depending on the brand of vaccine used, so don't be alarmed if your puppy is having the injections on a different timescale to others you know. It is important to follow your vet's advice on when to allow your pup to go to the park or to training classes or outside generally. Please note the puppy is allowed (even though he is not vaccinated) in your garden – a must in order to get the house-training going quickly (see 3.22 and 3.23). He can also go in the car – a must to get him used to travelling and he can go for walks in your arms, in a bag or a doggy buggy – he must not go on the floor outside of your property where other dogs have potentially been. I always do this with my young pups as it gets them used to 'life' straight away

2.6 Veterinary Health Checks, Oral Hygiene and Weight Control

Many veterinary surgeons offer six-monthly check-ups. These are to help prevent illness and are useful in terms of general healthcare, care of teeth and gums, and weight management. Toothbrushes are now available to clean teeth, with meat-flavoured toothpaste, no less! Checking and cleaning your pup's teeth is a useful habit to get into and it makes it 'the norm' for the dog's mouth to be examined (reducing stress if your vet has to look inside the mouth at any point). You also get to know what your pup's teeth are like and any abnormalities can be picked up on swiftly.

Toothache is very painful and all dentistry with dogs has to be done under a general anaesthetic. Giving a regular mix of items to chew and a good quality, well balanced diet (no sugary foods, drinks or junk foods – just like with kids), can help in the battle against tooth decay. There are now plenty of purpose-designed toys and chews on the market to help with this. Dry food helps to keep teeth clean – if your puppy is solely on wet food and you intend to keep him on it, consider providing regular alternatives for oral maintenance and teeth cleaning.

Regular visits to the vet can reduce the amount of stress your dog feels when he goes there. Taking him once a year for an injection can leave a bad impression on a dog, and perhaps make each visit more difficult for both of you. Routine visits to see a nurse for weighing and dietary advice, popping in for flea control and wormers and taking your dog with you for lots of fuss and a few treats, can make these trips less of a strain.

Overweight dogs are all around us you just have to look. As with humans a dog's general health is affected by being 'a porker', in some cases quite seriously. Reduce treats (or use low calorie alternatives such as raw veg), change the food to a light version – most brands of food have a low calorie range – and increase exercise *gradually*. Suddenly taking a dog for a two-hour run if he is only used to short walks may cause injury especially if he is overweight. And remember – over-feeding a dog is not being kind!

Feeling a dog to gauge weight is sometimes more accurate than scales. If the dog is at the right weight, you should be able to run your hands down its sides and count the ribs easily – but they should *not* be sticking out. If you have to dig around a bit to find them, your dog is overweight. The waist should be easily observed and nip in just in front of the hips. Underneath the dog, the chest should dip down and then the abdomen should tuck up neatly. The undercarriage should not go straight across – if it does, your dog is overweight. If you follow these three tips and keep your dog within these guidelines, you won't go far wrong weight-wise.

2.7 Worming and Flea Control

This is essential healthcare. You can't skimp on this. Puppies can become ill, irritable and very sore if these two elements are not maintained on a regular basis. Fleas like to live in houses and will often fester in your carpets, laying eggs and only hopping on the dog for an occasional feed. When treating for fleas it is crucial to treat the carpet, furniture and the animal's bedding. Sprays are available for this. There are many different cures or preventative treatments on the market. As they are in fact poisons, most treatments are available only from veterinary surgeons and must be given in accordance with the dog's age and size. Flea bites can cause quite a reaction, going on to cause skin infections and hair loss if not treated.

Puppies should be wormed every two weeks until twelve weeks old, then every month until six months of age. After six months a worming treatment should be given at least every three months throughout their lives, but this can vary hugely depending on the type of treatment. Speak to your veterinary practice regarding this issue to make sure your dog is properly covered.

I use a monthly chewable treatment that does both fleas and worms. Dead easy!

If a dog has worms it can lose weight, the tummy can become swollen, and it may be susceptible to bouts of diarrhoea or constipation. They can also act as though they've never been fed, the poor starving creatures – giving rise to owners changing food as the dog is not 'satisfied' – when in fact they are just worm-infested. Some life-threatening conditions are directly related to worm infestation. Recently a puppy owner enquired about changing food. Their dog, Megan, was suddenly starving all the time so I suggested increasing the amount given as she was growing and a sudden growth spurt can increase appetite. This made no difference and a week later they approached with the same enquiry. The suggestion of worms had them hot-footing it to their vets where a preparation was duly dispensed. The following week in class Megan was back to her old bouncy, but satisfied self – no longer starving – but of course refusing nothing on offer just the same. Typical!

Flea treatments usually begin when a puppy is two days old. There are special preparations. They come in a can that you spray on your hands and then wipe on the animal. From ten weeks old they can have a 'spot on' treatment which is a small amount of liquid poured onto the back of the neck.

These flea treatments should be used as described (which is regularly), not as and when you spot a flea! Most dogs hate to be sprayed with an aerosol can. The 'spot on' treatments cause most dogs no concern (although my spaniel Parsnip seriously disagrees with this comment, hence we use a chewable preparation) and are easy to apply. The majority of dogs will have a few fleas at some point in their lives. Good indicators are excessive scratching and little black bits (flea dirt) in their coats. You won't mistake a flea if you see it. It is small and dark and jumps away just when you go to pinch it between your nails. If left unchecked, a flea infestation can cause serious, itchy and painful skin problems potentially making the dog's skin very sensitive. The fleas can also have a nibble at us, giving us a few itchy spots to think about, although we don't really make for a satisfying meal.

Fleas quite like furniture and bedrooms to live in, and are not satisfied with staying around the dog's bedding area.

2.8 Giving Medication

You will, at some point in your dog's life, have to give him medication. Obviously this should only be done on the advice of your veterinary surgeon. Your vet or vet nurse will show you how to give the medication. They will also have many different ideas and approaches to this if you find it difficult. When in doubt – ask!

2.9 Administering Tablets

Tablets are the most common medication we have to give our dogs. They may be simple worming tablets or antibiotics to cure or prevent an infection.

You come home from the vet, and your dog eyes the bottle or package with suspicion. They don't miss much. Reaching into the fridge, you pull out some ham or cheese, arousing their immediate interest. You then struggle with the childproof lid on the bottle of pills. Pushing a pill into the cheese, you offer it tentatively to your dog – you're worried about whether he will or won't eat it. Eyeing you with some misgivings, he looks at the cheese, turns his nose up and walks away. He may even take the cheese, roll it around in his mouth until he has sucked it off, and then spit the tablet out at your feet. After three attempts, the dog is full of cheese or ham and the tablet is a soggy mess on the floor.

If your dog won't take tablets out of your hand and

just swallow them (and some greedy individuals do), then prepare three or four 'doctored' treats *out of their sight*. Give them the first bit, then immediately offer the second (this one should have the tablet in), following up straight away with the third and fourth bit. The tendency is for them to eat faster, or swallow whole, when there is something else on offer straight away.

If you want to pop the tablet straight down the throat, put the pill between your index and middle finger. Open the mouth by applying gentle pressure at the sides, and pop the tablet as far to the back as possible. Pull your fingers out (count them) and close the mouth. Gently hold the mouth closed, tilting the head slightly backwards, and stroke the throat. The only problem with this method is that if the dog tastes the pill, and it is disgusting, he may seriously object to you doing it again. Picking up the pill bottle sends him running for cover!

2.10 Cleaning Ears and Popping in Ear Drops

Dogs can have ear problems that require you to clean out their ears and apply drops. If their ears are sore, this can be a painful process – ears are very sensitive. To avoid a dog becoming unhappy about this procedure it helps to give nice food at the same time as the eardrops and cleaning is being done. This makes it a two-man job; at least for the first few times you do it.

Hold some food that the dog really likes in your hand. Allow the dog to lick at your hand and slowly release the food as the other person cleans the ears and pops in the drops. After a while, when the dog sees the ear cleaner and drops, he will come and sit waiting for them, knowing that a reward will soon follow. The same process can be used for eye drops, cleaning wounds, and many other 'uncomfortable' treatments we have to do to. Word to the wise – use good food. This is one time when a piece of dog food just won't cut it! Garlic sausage, cheese, cream cheese directly licked from the tube, you get the idea.

2.11 Cleaning Eyes and Administering Drops or Ointment

Most breeds of dog don't need their eyes cleaned, but there are a few that do. Notably bichon frisés, shih tzus and some cavalier King Charles spaniels. It is always advisable to seek veterinary advice if your dog's eyes are runny, irrespective of breed, until you get to know what is and what is not normal for your dog. I have a pug called Strumpet. Pugs are known for having eye trouble and she developed a weepy eye a few weeks after I acquired her. It was an ulcer on her eyeball (very painful) and she required special eye drops to settle it down. About two months later the other eye started weeping. The temptation was to use up the remainder of the eye drops that we already had, but thankfully I didn't. This time it was a melting ulcer, very serious, and she had to be transported to Birmingham for emergency surgery to save the eye.

It's always worth getting a vet to give the eye the once over!

For the persistent runny eye that is not any type of infection or injury (hairs are normally the culprit), regular cleaning is needed. Use warm water, a ball of cotton wool or a soft tissue and just gently wipe away the gunge. Do this every day or you might end up with crusty eyes where the gunge gets caught up in the hair underneath the eye (causing gunge lumps AKA eye bogies), and this can cause discomfort.

End each cleaning session with a nice treat so the puppy or dog feels happy to go through the process again. With small wriggly dogs it can help if someone holds them in their arms while you do the cleaning, or wait until they are tired and curled up next to you for a nap and just gently wipe the gunk away.

If eye drops or ointment need to be administered then follow the advice of your veterinary practice as to how much and how often. Then, choosing a time when your dog is calm and treats are to hand, ask your dog to sit. Hold the head gently (perhaps someone else could help) and open the eye slightly squirting or 'dropping' as you do. I always find the quicker, the better, with things like this. Give the tasty treat *immediately*. Try different locations if you are having difficulty. I tried many options with Strumpet (the pug) and opted for the kitchen work surface in the end. I put the treat on the opposite surface so she couldn't just keep making a grab for it (she is very greedy) and asked her to sit. As she was at my height it made the task quicker and simpler for me and no grabbing and pinning down was needed.

It doesn't matter what treatment you are giving, always follow it up with a tasty treat so the dog comes away feeling good about it. Also, minimal restraint is always better, so the dog doesn't feel threatened by the process. Start off this way with every puppy or dog to ensure they are happy with what is happening: It is a lot easier to do it this way than to sort out an unhappy, frightened or angry dog because you have been too heavy-handed in the beginning.

2.12 The Finances of Dog Ownership

There are many considerations to make when buying a puppy. Is my house and car big enough? Can I provide sufficient exercise? Will my family cope?

What about the financial aspect of owning a puppy?

The initial purchase price is just the beginning of a long-term financial commitment to caring for a dog. There isn't just the cost of feeding a good quality diet or providing a few little extras such as treats and toys. Fees for vaccinations and adequate and regular flea and worm control also add to the overall cost of keeping a dog. Add to that a decent health insurance policy (a must these days), a crate for the car, repairs to the car before the crate is bought, puppy and dog training classes – and you are looking at quite a hefty investment. Then, if you should have the good fortune to be able to take an annual holiday, don't forget to add in the cost of boarding kennels or a house sitter.

Getting a rescue dog is not necessarily a cheaper alternative. All of the above costs can be involved, with the exception of the purchase price, but you may need additional training or even behavioural advice. The difference is negligible.

Regarding insurance the ideal policy to look for is one that covers the dog for life, for any condition.

CHAPTER THREE

Birth to Three Months (ish)

3.1 Early Development

Puppies grow at an alarming rate. Most of them go from the human equivalent of nought to eighteen in just one year of their life. That is a very steep growth curve, in both physical and mental terms. For instance the small, highly dependent puppy turns into a temperamental teenager within a few months, with a mind of its own and sometimes attitude to match. Lessons learned in the early months, before puberty, can last the whole of our dogs' lifetime. We don't get this time again with them, so we should make the most of it.

3.2 Nought to Two Weeks

During this phase puppies are deaf and blind and totally dependent upon their natural mother. They have basic reflex actions – they can yelp or whine if distressed – but they cannot toilet without the mother stimulating them by licking their stomachs and bottoms. They can move, but only in circles. This is called 'rooting behaviour' and helps them find the 'milk bar'. Their sense of smell dictates which way to 'root'.

3.3 Two to Three Weeks

Now their eyes respond to light and movement and they can

hear. General movement is increased as the puppy learns to stand and move forwards and backwards.

3.4 *Three Weeks Plus*

At this stage, learning begins in earnest. With all five senses now working fully, puppies begin to show curiosity about their surroundings and interact with each other in play. They start to learn social skills and take notice of people and other animals.

At three to four weeks the mother begins the weaning process, an important life lesson for both species. Also around this time the mother begins to reduce the youngsters' dependency on her, and starts to teach them some life lessons – such as where the toilet is.

At seven to eight weeks of age, puppies start to show signs of fear and can be startled by new noises and sights. By providing new and different objects for them to explore, a radio to listen to and frequent, gentle handling from three weeks of age, this fear of the unknown is greatly reduced and the puppy learns to take things in its stride.

Introduce your puppy within its first fourteen weeks to other people, cats, guinea pigs and pets, as well as to the vacuum cleaner, lawnmower and car. This early education is critical in producing a well-balanced pup that can deal with everyday, as well as unique, situations. These early weeks are when the youngster learns about communication, how to interact effectively with both the family group and outsiders – and who and what to trust.

3.5 *Being Safe*

The period of confinement due to vaccinations interferes with this learning process, but there is little point in endangering your puppy by exposing it to the outside world before it is properly protected. Puppies can be taken out on car journeys, and carried around outside on walks, while friends and family can come and visit. The underlying principle is to encourage your pup's opportunities to see the world in frequent but short doses.

3.6 *Keep Introducing Them to New Things*

We should try not to shield our pup from new experiences, situations and objects. We cannot wrap them in cotton wool, and trying to do so may not help them in the long term. Fearful responses only get worse with age as the animal simply 'grows into' its fear, and being afraid becomes part of its personality or make-up. Even dogs of a year or more that have been properly raised at the breeders and in their new homes can lose the ability to cope with new individuals or situations if they are over-protected.

3.7 *What Can Happen if We Miss Out on These Early Weeks*

Puppies that have been kept in boring and isolated surroundings during this important early period may develop a tendency to overreact. A dog becomes too excitable on meeting new people and jumps up, barks, growls and backs away or pees on their feet. This could develop into aggressive or fearful behaviour. My trainers get peed on weekly in puppy school!

3.8 *Weaning – An Important Life Lesson*

Weaning not only transfers the young animal from liquid food to solids, but teaches an important emotional lesson: how to handle frustration! It is the puppy's first lesson in emotional 'toughening up'. In puppies the first sign of weaning is when the mother begins denying instant access to her teats by moving out of the way. This makes the puppies feel frustrated, and their first response is to try harder to get food by grabbing at the teats, holding on, and squealing when the mother walks away. The mother then returns and feeds the puppies as normal. This continues, but the delay between denying and feeding increases each time. Eventually the breeder will provide bowls of solid food for the hungry puppies. The mother is often removed from the pups at this time.

Hand-reared puppies tend not to go through this process. They are continually fed on demand and struggle to learn these early lessons. This can result in difficult adults with little or no emotional control – rather like spoiled children.

This is the same process our children go through although it's the supermarket or corner shop where you are most likely to observe the behaviour. The child wants sweets (typically two years old). The mother says no. The child kicks off like a rocket and sprawls on the floor, kicking and screaming. The mother who gives into the frustrated child will probably have difficulties whenever the child is denied something, whereas the mother that walks away will see her child transformed back to normal and racing after her once again all sweetness and light!

3.9 Preparing for Your Puppy

It is important to think through what your pup's needs will be when he is brought home. We need to be able to feed him, provide fresh water, somewhere to toilet and a cosy place to sleep – that means two bowls, a bed and a back yard. If we don't want him to play with our slippers, we must also think about giving toys. As we don't yet know the puppy's individual likes and dislikes, it might be worth buying something hard and something soft to play with; for example, a hard bone and a rope toy. You can extend the range of toys when you discover what his preferences are.

Puppies need to learn quickly to toilet in the garden and have somewhere to 'let off steam'. Ensuring your garden is secure and safe for your puppy should be done before he moves in, to avoid accidents and escape-artist antics. There are going to be toileting accidents in the first few weeks so a specialised cleaning product is a good thing to have handy in the cupboard. You can get this from your vet or local pet shop. If not, biological washing powder and surgical spirit will serve (see section 3.22 and 3.23).

In the first few days feed the same diet as at the breeders: this avoids upset stomachs and provides a little continuity for the puppy. The breeder will probably sell you a small supply to start with. It is then worth talking to your veterinary surgeon or knowledgeable pet store about the best food for your puppy. If the breeder gives you a long list of foods such as cereals for breakfast, something else for lunch etc. then I would ignore this and get a decent puppy food instead.

It's a good idea to buy a carry cage or crate, especially if collecting your puppy involves a car journey. Many young animals are sick or toilet in the car on their first journey home, so you may not want them on your lap. Kitchen roll, wet wipes and air freshener are essential on this journey.

3.10 Setting Your Ground Rules

A puppy really wants to please its new 'parent', and this is the basis of our extraordinary relationship with them. As with all 'children' it is imperative that they get guidance from us in how to behave. Ground rules or boundaries are essential for harmony in the home. Deciding in advance what rules you are going to set for your dog avoids having to correct them at a later date. These decisions are personal to your situation and could be discussed with the whole family so everyone is in agreement.

Your house rules should include where you are going to allow your dog in the house. Is he going to be allowed on the furniture and upstairs, and where is he going to sleep at night? There is no sensible reason for refusing to let dogs sleep on the bed or get on the sofa, other than that these areas are easily soiled and we use them too! Allowing them on our furniture, which smells so reassuringly of us, does not make them believe they control the house (see 1.5 and 1.7), but there are practical issues to consider. For example, if your puppy is a particularly hairy or large breed, you may want him to sleep somewhere other than your bed. For hygiene reasons, you may want to discourage him from jumping up at kitchen surfaces or sitting in the middle of the dining table! Dogs don't really understand 'being muddy', so free access at all times to the settee could be a problem. In these cases it may be worth going down the 'invitation only' route: the dog can only get up on the sofa when invited. A special blanket placed on the settee is a really easy method. Put the blanket on the sofa and invite the dog up. If he tries to get up when the blanket is not there, push him off. Most dogs very quickly get the idea.

To some people the whole purpose of a dog is to have a constant companion who goes everywhere, while others may want a more structured relationship. What we need to do as 'parents' is to be clear in our own minds what we expect from our dog. Set our ground rules and stick to them. True and unwavering consistency is the only real key to achieving the harmony at home that comes from solid boundaries (see 4.16). But be sure that the boundaries decided upon are realistic. For example, a Labrador puppy is small, fluffy and cute, but it's unrealistic to allow this puppy to jump up while he's little, then expect him to 'know' when he is too big to do so. Equally, to allow a German shepherd puppy to sleep beside you on the bed might be lovely, but when he is fully grown – you ain't all gonna fit!

Puppies don't have much respect for newly landscaped gardens. Everything to them is new and requires further investigation, sometimes to the point of nibbling or digging up interesting items (see 6.12). Fencing off parts of the garden and allowing only supervised visits to them may be worth considering. And if you like a tidy house, everyone in the family should agree to put shoes, remote controls, mobile phones and all other items of value that could be interesting to your puppy away or out of reach! (See 3.24.)

3.11 Bringing Your Puppy Home

Finally, with all preparations made, the house tidied, the garden resembling Colditz, the travel crate in the car and the dog's new possessions unpacked and in place, it is time to collect 'the beastie' from the breeder. Most breeders do not feed the puppy just before it is collected, to reduce mishaps in the car. However, it is worth taking towels, wet wipes, plastic bags and some cleaning product along with you, especially if the journey is long. Take along water in a bottle, and a small bowl so the puppy can be offered something to drink on a long journey.

On getting home, take the puppy straight into the back garden and wait with him until he has relieved himself. This is crucial and starts the toilet training off on the right track (see 3.22). Once he has 'been', show him where the water bowl is. Then introduce him to his bed or sleeping area and place toys in this vicinity. Stay calm and keep everything as low-key as possible: this helps the puppy to acclimatise to his new circumstances with the minimum of fuss. Allow him to explore the areas of your house that you want him to have access to. Be kind and attentive – this is an important day for all of you – the bonding starts here!

The first meal could be a complete disaster. The puppy

won't eat, or has gone behind the washing machine and won't come out. No matter. Some pups may be completely overawed with new people, a new house, and no mother or siblings. They might hide for hours, refuse to eat or keep their distance from you. This is to be expected. The whole world the dog knows has been turned on its head. He needs time and space to gather his thoughts and take in all the changes. Food could be the last thing on his mind. Do you feel hungry when you are very unsettled? Most of us lose our appetites for a while in a life-changing situation. The best approach is to do nothing regarding the puppy and carry on cooking the dinner, watching the television or reading a book until he decides to take part. Dragging him out from his hidey-hole behind the settee could increase the distress and make him afraid. Try not to be tempted.

3.12 Dealing with Fear

Fear can be learned in a split second, and take many days, weeks, months or even years to unlearn. Reactions to fearful situations can vary among different species, but they are typically based on one of the four F's: fight, flight, freeze, and flirt. Puppies and dogs can shake, pant, dig, growl, bite, bark, look cute, roll over, run around or pee themselves. Having moved into a new situation your dog will no doubt come across objects, noises and maybe even people he is afraid of. Our reaction to that fear can mould the animal's view of what scared him, and alter what he does in the future.

Consider a child crying because they are afraid of thunder. We would sit the child on our knee, give them a cuddle and dry their tears, all the time explaining to them why there was nothing to be scared of. This could be a complex explanation of electrical discharge, cloud formation and atmospherics in an attempt to send the child to sleep, or an intricate story of friendly giants playing skittles in the sky. Reassurance is what we are aiming for, through talking to them in a way they can understand.

Now, consider doing the same to a puppy or dog. Not having the ability to understand what we are saying, they read the situation entirely differently. Cuddling, stroking, or even just eye contact with the puppy (or dog) when he is afraid can say directly to him 'you are right to be frightened'. He might even think that we are afraid too! The outcome is that the fear is confirmed, and the puppy will probably be even more scared the next time. This is one of the areas where our dogs differ so much from us. We can rationalise fear through speech – they cannot. Our behaviour in these situations forms their future reactions.

We need to stay calm and not react, look at or talk to our dog in the seconds after the scary event. Dogs do not exist for us in those few short (excruciatingly difficult) moments. We must carry on as though absolutely nothing has happened. This is tough – as we care strongly about how our dogs feel, and want to look after them – but well worth it!

This simple technique can avoid a phobia forming. We learn to be afraid, and then we unlearn it. A phobia forms when the unlearning process does not happen, and the fear escalates out of proportion. Typical doggy phobias can be fireworks, thunder, crow scarers, flies and even black plastic bin-bags. Noise phobias are very difficult to live with and can cause a great deal of distress throughout the dog's life. Definitely something we want to avoid.

3.13 Managing Fear

If a dog has already become afraid, we have to do as advised above but also try and help them cope. Natural calming remedies such as Serene-UM, Zylkene and Pet Remedy diffusers and sprays given / used daily can be very useful in stressful situations, getting the dog to relax and manage its emotions. These are available from good pet stores and veterinary practices and are safe to give to any age of puppy or dog. Giving the dog somewhere to hide in the house – an indoor kennel, a cardboard box or a coffee table with blankets draped over it – can provide an easily accessible den where he feels safe. Sometimes simple distraction techniques work well. Giving a dog a big juicy bone might take his mind off a thunderstorm. Playing with a toy that is special (like a squeaky) that only comes out at these times may help. Neither of these techniques will increase the fear, so there is no risk of worsening the problem. The dog will not engage in the activity if he is very afraid.

Something else to consider is a Thundershirt. This specially designed T-shirt is like a pressure wrap that helps keep dogs calm by applying pressure to the torso. It sounds simple and it is. It is also very effective and well worth a try. All you have to do at the first sign of your dog becoming stressed or afraid is put the shirt on, wrap it round and fasten the Velcro fittings.

There are CDs that play noises such as fireworks, loud bangs and thunder, and using one of these can be helpful (it can be used in conjunction with the Thundershirt and something like Serene-UM for maximum effect). Play it at a low volume until the dog can cope with the sound, and then steadily increase the volume as he learns to manage. Be busy when you do this so you are not tempted to sit and stare at the dog. Read a book or do housework, anything that keeps you occupied. Maybe offer him a special chew at this time to enhance the experience. Over days and weeks this can reduce the fear. Of course the noise comes from speakers, so this may not help in a 'real' situation, but if applied properly, there is no risk to this approach and it is worth trying. I have found that it can, at the very least, reduce the shock factor. The trick is to go very slowly with the volume button, increasing it by only a notch per week, but play the CD for as much as two hours per day.

3.14 Introducing Pets to Each Other

The following sections are about introducing a very young dog to an older pet already living in the house. If you are introducing a puppy to an older dog or cat it needs to be done at home, preferably in the garden. But introducing two adult dogs is best done outside, in the local park or at the rescue centre, as opposed to on your own property (see 8.4). Section 3.17 deals with introducing a kitten to an adult dog or slightly older puppy. Young puppies and kittens will typically just play with each other, making the introduction simple and self-explanatory.

3.15 Introducing a Puppy to an Older Dog

The introduction should be made as soon as the puppy comes home, and preferably in the garden. The puppy could be loose on the grass, and the older dog on a loose lead. Allow them to sniff each other. Don't be concerned if the older dog rolls the puppy onto its back to sniff and lick its genitals and stomach, this is normal. Be careful where the older dog puts its feet, as some can have a tendency to be a little rough. If the older dog does pin the puppy down with its foot, call him off or distract him away using a toy. Try not to pull on the lead as this can make the older dog annoyed (being physically pulled away from something interesting can be very irritating and we want this greeting to be nice for everyone). Difficulties can sometimes arise if the older dog feels jealous of the newcomer. We can overcome this by ensuring the older dog gets as much love and attention as before and the puppy does not become the exclusive focus of everyone's attention.

Being over-protective of the puppy and continually telling the older dog off for going near him will cause problems. The older dog will undoubtedly begin to view the puppy as a prelude to punishment, and may not want him around. Close supervision between the two is advised in the first few days, as they need to learn to share the house, toys, beds and you! Avoid unnecessary conflict by keeping them separated in those first few days when unsupervised. Your older dog may need time and space away from the irritating, bouncy puppy, and the puppy needs to rest and conserve some energy in order to grow and develop. Spending time with the puppy away from the older dog ensures the nurturing bonding takes place with you – and not solely with him!

3.16 Introducing a Puppy to a Cat

Cats usually run when threatened. Dogs naturally chase moving targets. This is the main difficulty you face in this situation. Introducing the puppy to the cat is better if the puppy is tired, and not bounding around. Carrying the cat into the room restricts its natural flight instinct, and you may get scratched or bitten. It may be better to allow this encounter to happen naturally, without it being too staged. The cat needs somewhere to bolt to, and if the puppy chases it a swift scratch on the nose can teach the puppy a valuable lesson about felines. A cat with previous experience of dogs may not run away at all, and most puppies will approach a static cat tentatively, and then try and initiate play. Do not be surprised if your cat moves into the garden or upstairs for a few days or weeks. These things have a habit of resolving themselves without too much intervention from us – each individual will find its level with the other. If a puppy becomes intensely aggressive on sight of a cat (and this does happen but is quite rare), then this does not bode well for good relations. Keeping them entirely separate for their lifetime is difficult. Cats do have a habit of voting with their feet and moving to another house!

An indoor kennel can provide a place where your puppy can see the cat, but cannot chase it. This won't stop the puppy from becoming highly excited on seeing the cat, and chasing it at the next available opportunity. Use gates across doorways so the puppy has to stop and the cat can get away to safety. Sometimes having a lead on the puppy whenever the cat is about works well. Tie the lead around your waist or wrist (don't do this with strong adult dogs for obvious reasons). This stops the chase behaviour immediately and the puppy gets used to just pottering around behind you and over time the puppy can learn to ignore the cat. Interrupting any attempts to chase by doing some swift training with tasty treats (see Chapter Five) can also help distract the puppy.

3.17 Introducing a Kitten to an Adult Dog or Older Puppy

Dogs are natural hunters of big or small furry things. Some can have a strong urge to hunt, while others have no urges at all. Most dogs fall into the in-between category, where they will chase at full speed, catch up with their 'prey' and then have no idea what to do next. If your dog is a hunter that follows the 'pounce/bite/kill' sequence, then do not get a kitten.

There will be great excitement from the dog when you bring the kitten home. A new toy, one that moves and makes noises! But kittens can bite and scratch. A couple of nips to the nose, or a kitten clinging on with its claws to the muzzle, is often enough to restrain an over-zealous dog. Introducing a dog to a kitten after a long walk and a full meal will reduce the excitement levels naturally. If the kitten is timid, and hiding behind the bath panels, keep the dog away from the area. Having a huge slobbering muzzle sniffing frantically at the entrance to the kitten's bolthole is not helpful in making a kitten relax and feel at home.

If you put the kitten on the floor and allow the dog to sniff it all over, you may arouse hunting instincts that you've never seen before. The dog needs to learn that this is a new addition to his family. Hold the kitten on your knee, and allow the dog to come up and sniff and lick the kitten. If the kitten is quite relaxed, release the strength of your hold on him, so he can begin to interact with the dog.

Common sense dictates that the dog should not be allowed to stand on the kitten or to play roughly with it, because the kitten can be easily hurt. Parental supervision is required!

3.18 Settling Down for the Night

The first night in a new home can be traumatic for a puppy. He has lost siblings and familiar surroundings, and has never been alone in his very short life. Isolation is distressing unless you are used to it. Most youngsters weep and wail in their first few nights. They may cry for a short period, then fall asleep, only to wake again two hours later and let rip! There are various actions we can take. We can ignore the puppy, put earmuffs on, and hope the neighbours understand. In most cases, a few nights of not reacting to his cries will make him stop. However, some pups are quite resilient, and can keep going with their yowling. If we give up and go down to them, the strategy has worked. They will do it again and again, because they have learned that howling fetches 'Mummy'.

A less stressful approach might be to allow him to sleep upstairs in an indoor kennel or travel crate for the first few nights, while he is settling in and getting to know you and his new surroundings. Most youngsters will sleep soundly, knowing you are close by. The crate ensures he doesn't get onto the bed, or into any mischief, and it also contains any toilet accidents. As puppies are less likely to soil their nest, he will probably wake you if he needs to go to the toilet, keeping your house-training on track.

Once he is settled into the house (and the indoor kennel), move the crate to where you want him to sleep. Leave a side light on in the room, and a radio on low to keep him as calm and stress-free as possible. If you are happy to keep him in the bedroom, you need do nothing.

Having a set routine at bedtime helps the puppy to understand what is going on. For instance put him out for a last pee and pop two or three biscuits into his kennel or bed. When he comes in the treats are there, waiting for him. Keep the bedtime cuddles to a minimum to reduce the emotional upset of being left.

A Pet Remedy diffuser can help at this time. Simply switch it on in the room your puppy is to sleep in a few minutes before you put him to bed. Turn it off in the morning.

3.19 Leaving Your Puppy

Our dogs need to cope without us being there all the time. We cannot be on call 24/7. The earlier we begin to leave a dog alone, the quicker he will catch on that we are coming back. Simple things like shutting the loo door to stop him following you everywhere can be enough to start this learning process. Nipping out to the post box down the street – leaving him completely alone in the house for a full five minutes – is something to start doing *straight away*. Try not to make the mistake of spending the first week continually with the puppy, as this will make leaving harder – especially for him!

Gradually increase the length of time the puppy is left. Keep the goodbyes and hellos low-key. Some dogs or puppies greet us as though we have been away for hours, when in fact it was seconds. Say a swift hello, and carry on about your business in a matter of fact way to show the puppy there is no big deal here. Fond and lengthy farewells increase the neediness of the puppy at that particular moment. We are saying, 'Bye baby, Mummy won't be long, you be a good puppy' while stroking him fondly. He is thinking and feeling, 'Please don't leave me, please don't go'. Emotions are ruffled and he can feel bereft.

Two treats in the bed or indoor kennel, a swift pat on the head, turn and walk out the door. Try not to look back. Short and to the point is kinder than drawn out and emotional. The treats are compensation for losing you for a while (and if you do the same thing at bedtime it helps with all round consistency). They also become a signal to the puppy or dog that there will be no further 'parental' contact for a while.

Leaving a radio on low reduces the feelings of isolation and cuts down the noises from outside and the creaking and cracking sounds of an empty house. These noises can be a bit scary to a solitary dog. They're noises he probably wouldn't even notice if you were there.

3.20 Teaching Your Puppy About His Crate

Indoor kennels, crates and doggy dens are different terms for the same thing – a lockable cage that a puppy can be put into. This sounds cruel, and admittedly it does lend itself to misuse, but when introduced and used correctly the crate is a place of sanctuary and safety. It is somewhere the puppy or dog chooses to go into for a rest, or to avoid the kids for a while. Somewhere a puppy can be holed up for a couple of hours so you can do other things and know he is safe and not chewing through live electrical wires. Misuse is often along the lines of locking a puppy or adult dog in for ten hours a day, or not introducing them properly to the den so that it becomes a punishment place and not a safety zone.

To introduce a puppy to the doggy den begin by putting it

in an accessible place and placing his bedding and some toys inside. At meal times put the food bowl or food-dispensing toys (see 4.22) inside the den so he begins to eat his meals in there. Don't shut the door until the puppy starts to go to his crate for naps and is comfortable with being inside. Then close the door for a few minutes. Allow him out *before* he becomes upset about being confined. It can take anything from a few hours to several days for a puppy to feel at home in his crate. Once he is comfortable we can begin leaving him for longer periods. (Introducing an older dog to a crate can take longer.)

The uses of crates go beyond simply keeping the puppy safe while you are out. An over-excited puppy can be calmed down by placing him in his crate for a sleep with a nice chew bone or biscuit (see 4.18). The crate can be placed in the car to make car travel less stressful – the puppy feels better because he is in his crate (see 6.20). The puppy can also be taken anywhere. Barbecues, friends' houses, hotels, lecture theatres – many people who attend my lectures bring their dogs and they sit quite happily in their crates.

If a young dog is left for many hours in his crate he may grow to resent it and become morose and sullen when put in there. Alternatively, he may start creating and trying to noisily dig his way out. Two to three hours is considered an appropriate time as long as he is fed and exercised beforehand.

My pug, Strumpet, spent too much of her early life in a crate: indeed this was the reason for her being re-homed. I got her at ten months old and she came complete with two indoor kennels. Having been told she was crate trained I decided to take her to one of my lectures the next day (where dogs have to be crated). I arrived and took her in and while my colleague made much of her I fetched her crate. Within two minutes of being in the crate she wet herself. She stood, head down, making strange little pug type noises for the next forty minutes. She was grief-stricken and shaking. So, breaking all the rules we had her out and played pass the pug for the rest of the day. Needless to say I haven't taken her with me again and thankfully I don't have need to crate her.

3.21 Grooming and Health Checks

Certain breeds of dog need more grooming than others. Without exception they all need to be checked over at some point for ear problems, sore paws, irritations around the tail – so they all need to be comfortable with being checked over and perhaps being brushed or combed.

From day one of owning a puppy we should be checking him regularly, perhaps twice per day when he is sitting comfortably beside us or on our laps. Feel down his back, check his bottom, gently examine between his toes, open up his mouth to see his teeth, and glance into his ears. We need to make this a pleasant experience. There is little point in doing this exercise when he is rowdy and playful: he will only give us a hard time. When the pup is soppy and relaxed is the most obvious time. Your puppy will want to be beside you, and he is lying there because he wants some fuss. Just check him while fussing him!

The same goes for grooming. Trying to battle with a puppy for supremacy of the brush is a pointless exercise. As quickly as we wrestle it from his mouth, he has grabbed it again. Gently brushing him as he lays in a half-doze on the settee beside us gets him used to it quickly and with the minimum of fuss. Once he is happy for family members to do this, it is a good idea to get friends to do the same – just in case they ever have to. This all makes the groomer and veterinary surgeon's job easier, and visits to the vet less stressful, as the puppy is used to being touched all over by humans.

3.22 *Toilet Training*

Firstly, it must be said that your puppy is allowed into your garden. When you hear 'keep your puppy in until he has had all his jabs', please take that to mean keep him on your property – no excursions into the big wide world (unless you carry him). If you don't take him into the garden then he will quickly learn to pee and poo in your house and this becomes a hard habit to break.

Some basic facts: dogs are naturally clean animals, preferring to soil outside their immediate area. This is not due to an innate desire for a clean and tidy home, but has its roots in evolutionary history. A mother with young is very vulnerable, and in the wild the den is chosen carefully in order to keep the location as unobtrusive as possible. This would be futile if the scent of the den transmitted its presence like a flashing neon light. A clean den is an area relatively free of scent, so increasing the likelihood of the survival of the young (i.e. the pups don't get eaten!). The removal of all excretions from the young also reduces the potential for disease and parasitic infection, ensuring the general health of the litter.

In the first two weeks of life all excretions from puppies are stimulated directly by their mother licking their undersides. Once the puppies begin to move they are taken out of the whelping box regularly in order to play and investigate. As the majority of excretions occur when the puppy is wide awake and moving around, they happen more often away from the box, and the trigger for toileting becomes established as a particular type of flooring or grass. All poos and pees within the box continue to be cleaned away by the mother. This is toilet training 'doggy style' and is crucial for future development. The biological mother has done the early work for us and it is up to us to continue in the same relaxed manner. The upside is you can use kitchen roll or wet wipes to do it!

Take the puppy to the garden regularly – every hour to begin with – and use gentle praise when a performance is given. This way, toilet training is learned quickly and without fuss. This does not mean putting the puppy out and leaving him, as he may simply roam around the garden, dig a few holes, chew up your plants and then come back in and pee at your feet. He may just sit and whine at the back door. By accompanying the puppy it is possible to keep him calm and free from stress while also ensuring he does his business before you allow him back in. Most young puppies toilet after eating, sleeping and playing so it's a good idea to take them outside after such activities. An agitated appearance or sniffing and circling are excellent signs to watch for. The puppy swiftly makes a connection between being outside and going to the toilet and the type of surface he is on. Grass, gravel or concrete can then become a trigger for going to the toilet, coupled with the puppy's scent in the area – a bit like when we see a sign for the loo, it can make us want to go. By giving a gentle word signal, such as 'wee-wees', as soon as a puppy crouches to perform, they can be quickly taught to toilet when asked which is great if you are on a schedule.

This method of toilet training is not only quick and safe, but also encourages the puppy to toilet in one area in the garden or yard. If the puppy goes to the toilet indoors and it is not noticed for a while, it should be cleared away without any further reference. Don't clean up in front of the puppy. The mess should be viewed as our mistake – for not being vigilant – not the pup's. Better supervision will reduce the chances of it happening again. There is no real need for wild praise or food rewards while toilet training, as the relief felt by going to the toilet is a reward in itself. Saying 'good boy' is often enough.

A puppy squatting indoors can be quickly distracted with a hand clap or sharp 'No!', then taken outside to finish off. Our emotions should be kept to a minimum when doing this. We know from scientific research that punishment needs to be during the event, in order for a dog to understand why it is being told off (see 4.14 and 4.15). Dragging a reluctant puppy to a pile of mess and punishing him is counter-productive. The puppy learns that if there is a mess on the floor we are not happy, but won't make the connection of making the mess in the first place. This is where confusion and loss of confidence in the 'parent' can begin, and it will make the whole house-training process take much, much longer. To avoid potential problems in later months and years, and to promote a strong nurturing relationship, it would seem most sensible to follow the methods used by the biological mother, and train the puppy to toilet away from the den in the way nature intended.

Toilet training is an area where consistency is paramount. It will take several weeks, sometimes a bit longer – but there is no quick fix, so don't be tempted to chop and change what you do, rub his nose in it, shout and scream. All you'll end up doing is making it all take longer and wrecking your carpets in the process.

Puppy training pads and newspaper also prolong the process and are not recommended – very strongly not recommended. Essentially you are taking time-out to teach your puppy to toilet indoors when you really want him to go outside, which seems fairly pointless. And it can add weeks onto your house-training. Some dogs become so accustomed to the puppy pad that they simply won't go out for a toilet and come indoors to use the pad. Be very careful if you are using pads or paper and do not use them after the pup is eleven weeks old. Personally I would never bother.

3.23 Cleaning Up Accidents

Scent can draw a dog back to the wrong place to go to the toilet. Their remarkable sense of smell can pick up the finest remnants of previous toilets, and the dog or puppy can assume (rightly or wrongly) that this is the place to go. There are special products available from veterinary practices and good pet stores to properly clean away pees and poos. While this may on the surface appear to be another way of fleecing you of your hard earned dosh, there are good reasons why washing-up liquid and many disinfectants are not suitable. They may clear the toilet of what offends your sense of smell, but dogs have a far greater 'nose' than we do. Pheromones in their toilet are quite difficult to get rid of, and these are what attract our dogs. If you do not want to use a specialised cleaning product, then soak up as much pee as you can with kitchen towel. Clean the area thoroughly with a solution of biological washing powder made up at the correct temperature to activate it (see washing instructions on the packet). Soak up any remaining fluid, and then use a dab of surgical spirit to wipe the area completely clean. The enzymes in the biological washing powder break down the pheromones, then the pure alcohol cleans the area completely (do not be tempted to swig as you swab). What a faff! It's easier to just buy the pee cleaner instead.

And don't forget the poos. These fine specimens also get coated in pheromones on the way out so you do need to clean this area as well, even if there is no 'smudge'.

If your puppy or dog is toileting in the house in the same place then you are probably not cleaning up effectively.

3.24 Puppy Chewing Issues

Preventing a puppy from chewing is part of house-training. Going back to the question of punishment (a sharp 'No!'

or time-out see 4.14), we know that it has to be swift and immediate in order for a dog to understand and associate what it has done with the punishment that follows (see 4.14 and 4.15). To punish a puppy long after it has finished munching a favourite pair of slippers is pointless and counterproductive. On the other hand, to punish him while he has his teeth sunk into the slippers makes sense to the puppy if the punishment is swift and short-lived. As with toilet training, behaviour problems can occur later if punishment is too harsh and, more importantly, too late.

There is a vast range of toys now available for dogs in all shapes and sizes and with a variety of textures and tastes. A good variety of toys is important for a puppy as their natural instinct is to explore and experiment with different objects using their eyes, sense of smell, and of course touch. As with babies, everything goes in the mouth at this age.

The desire to chew is natural for a dog, especially for a teething puppy, and is a vital function for healthy teeth and gums. It is not the act of chewing that causes problems it is what the puppy decides to chew that irritates owners. Preventing chewing problems in a young puppy is simple. Give them access to plenty of chewable toys, and when they pick up something they should not play with (the TV remote is quite common), they should be told firmly 'No!' The puppy should then be given something he is allowed to chew and praised for showing interest. Keep all valuables out of the puppy's reach. This is a routine to adopt while the puppy is young and still learning the house rules. Following this strategy only once or twice will not curb the pup's natural curiosity, so as with toileting you need to be consistent for weeks and not keep chopping and changing your strategy. Try and ignore your puppy for 30 seconds after saying No! This provides a disconnect with what happened then and what happens now so we are not mistakenly rewarding the pup for thieving our stuff.

It is important to signal to the puppy what not to chew while giving him a good alternative. If an interesting pair of fluffy slippers is removed from a puppy, and a basic bone offered instead, the puppy may well feel cheated in that the bone is not very exciting and he may not be interested. The puppy may then try and recapture the slippers, or find something else of equal interest. The replacement should be chosen wisely from the selection of dog toys so as to offer something similar in texture and shape.

To recap, say 'No!' firmly. Ignore for 30 seconds (no eye contact) and then root through the toy box for a suitable alternative.

3.25 Puppy Play Biting

Many puppies enjoy chewing at their owners' hands and this could be described as a loving gesture when the puppy is very young. But their teeth are like needles and draw blood quickly, and it soon becomes more painful and unpleasant as the jaw muscles gain in strength. A puppy needs to learn that us humans are very delicate. If he puts his teeth anywhere near flesh, it hurts! In the litter, young puppies play by rough and tumbling and biting each other. When a bite is too hard the 'victim' will yelp and the game will finish. This teaches the puppy when to soften his bite: essentially the fun stops if the bite is too hard.

Take this life lesson in two stages. If you try and stop the play biting in one fell swoop your puppy won't learn to control his bite and every interaction you have will end up in mutual frustration.

1. When your puppy uses his teeth on you and applies pressure, say a high pitched 'Ouch' and walk away or stop the game. It may take a couple of weeks for the

puppy to generally nibble more softly or just mouth you softly with no teeth at all.

2. Then we can use the same technique to stop the biting altogether. Say 'Ouch' in the same way each and every time your puppy's teeth touch you, irrespective of how hard. Consistency and patience is all that is required.

The dog learns to control its jaw pressure, and if it is ever put in the position where it needs to bite, he will more likely use a soft bite than a bite that causes damage, because we have continued to help him learn to control his bite. For the majority of breeds these lessons need to be learned within the first three to four months of life.

Now, there are puppies that become frustrated with this method and start dive-bombing you with teeth gnashing and a crazy glint in their eyes. Time-outs work really well for these chaps. Simply say 'No!' and ignore for 30 seconds. If the pup comes straight back at you then put the puppy in another room or outside for two minutes. After two minutes open the door, walk away and ignore for 30 seconds (so you don't reward the punishment). This is obviously more labour-intensive for you and much less fun for the puppy than the method above, but it works really well for these individuals. The time-out allows the puppy to calm down a little, while the simple act of being 'cut off' from the group shows we are not happy. You do not need to shout with this method. In fact the calmer and more matter of fact you are, the more effective it is.

Play biting is a normal stage of development. Almost all puppies do it and your puppy is not abnormal if he is hurting you, certainly not aggressive. If he is play biting excessively at certain times of the day, particularly evenings then take a look at section 2.3.

CHAPTER FOUR

Three to Six Months (ish)

4.1 Important Times

Between three and six months our puppies develop quickly. This is a crucial period in their upbringing – it helps them to become well-balanced family members. They will have completed their vaccination courses and started to explore the big wide world. Some puppies grow ever more cheeky and confident with us at home, but may be frightened outside. Others can be as bold as brass wherever they are. The things we do at this stage in their life can mould our pups' behaviour, creating adults that are a pleasure to live with.

4.2 Making Friends

We all know that puppies need to socialise with other dogs, other animals (if they are going to come in contact with them regularly) and people. Walkies is the time for this. Meeting people, children and other dogs out on walks is an essential part of a puppy's upbringing. The way the puppy greets others is important to achieving a successful outcome and another friend made. Jumping all over other dogs and humans is not nice and frankly just plain rude. Work on this aspect of your puppy's behaviour from the first outing and he will be a firm favourite amongst the neighbourhood (see 5.11 Stopping Jumping Up).

The trick here is to teach the puppy to sit (see 5.4) every time you stop and speak to someone or greet another dog, so your puppy learns not to launch on them. A wayward puppy crawling on top of and jumping around their faces irritates many adult dogs. People you meet may stop to greet your puppy but quickly move on when they are literally wearing him. And beware of those people who say 'I don't mind', and encourage your puppy's 'kangaroo' behaviour. Remember he is your responsibility and take charge of the situation.

Puppy school is an excellent way for your puppy to make more doggy friends and learn about behaving well in a group situation. Good puppy classes are more than just training once a week - they are social gatherings with an educational edge. They offer you support, up-to-date information on healthcare, guidance on diet, tips on house training and how to get your pup to take worming tablets. They offer playtime with other puppies as well as other people and their children. Seemingly simple tasks such as teaching your puppy to sit calmly next to other puppies is harder than you think and this is a great time and place to practice.

4.3 What to Avoid In a Puppy School

Classes that meet for one hour a week and allow puppies to run around like lunatics run the risk of creating problems. A one-hour 'free for all' is not teaching puppies how to behave in social situations or a domestic environment. One common problem with this type of class is bullying. A puppy learns to bowl over other puppies and stand on them. He finds it fun and then tries the technique out on an adult dog in the park! He can then get a nasty shock when the dog says 'No' very forcefully. The bully's victim can also learn that playing with other dogs is unpleasant, and he can become afraid of approaching them. Or the puppy may learn that playing with other dogs is much more fun than listening to 'parents'.

Pups learn to ignore us quickly enough without giving them a forum in which to do it.

4.4 Finding a Reputable Puppy School

A good puppy school offers structured classes with set times for play, learning, and relaxing. The play sessions are monitored, with pups carefully assessed to avoid them being bullied, and to ensure that timid puppies gain in confidence. Training should be with treats or dog food, and there shouldn't be a choke chain in sight. If you have any questions the school should make time to answer them.

It is well known that stress slows down learning, both in dogs and humans, so a relaxed and fun place is what you should look for, with friendly and approachable people running it. Check what is available in your area and go along without your puppy. Don't take anyone else's word for it – see for yourself what the school is like, and take it from there.

4.5 Communication

Communication is the single most important element in a happy social group. If you look at your own family or workplace, it is often the person who cannot communicate their intentions or emotions clearly that causes the most unrest.

It's easy to communicate within your own species. We humans use the spoken word for direct communications, and the written word for more complex messages, though these can also be relayed via TV, internet and radio. We also take note of body language: we look at people's general demeanour and assess, for example, whether they are unhappy or just deep in thought. Dogs also read body language – each other's and ours. This can tell them whether or not it is safe to approach, and if play or another form of social interaction is on offer.

4.6 *Body Language*

The dog's body language can range from a mere widening of the eyes to a full full-scale body wag. It depends on breed-type and personality: there is no set code, though the position of tail and ears is important. This is one reason dogs should mix regularly with others, so their social skills can be practised and improved. The rottweiler, for example, has a thick, heavy frame that does not lend itself easily to understated movements. With its proud muzzle and flopped-over ears, the rottie's signalling elements are not very subtle. By contrast, the alert ears and erect tail of a Japanese Akita, which stand very straight and stiff, can look threatening to a dog not fluent in canine signalling. Easier-to-read breeds include German shepherds and Jack Russell terriers, whose upright ears can be a sign of interest, alarm, or threat. When their ears are back and flat, they signal fear, a generally flirtatious nature, uncertainty, or even ecstasy. The same range of emotions can be interpreted by the up or down tail position, and whether it is wagging or not. There is no set pattern to body language. We have to consider the animal's personality and take note of the dog's situation to correctly assess how it is feeling.

A dog who feels afraid could have its ears flattened against its head, but this could also mean it is flirting, trying to look cute to pacify someone, or that it's immensely happy and excited about something. A tucked-under tail and arched back can signify an extremely fearful dog, or it could be about to do the 'wall of death' around the living room, to burn off excess energy. Holding its body close to the ground can mean it is frightened, or that it is beginning its hunting sequence, starting with eye and going on to stalk and chase. One of my dogs, Strumpet (a black pug), has the ability to put on a 'mardy' expression (moody to those of you outside Leicester) at will, because it gets her lots of attention, particularly with my kids. I only know if she is really feeling upset by being aware of what's going on around her.

Some dogs smile, pulling their lips back to reveal glistening canines, which can be slightly unsettling if you don't know what is happening. If he's happy, his general body language should be excited and relaxed – if not, don't smile back!

Piglet, my husband's terrier (terrorist), smiles. I remember vividly the first time he did it. He was on my lap and we were having a nose to nose when suddenly I was subjected to a flash of pearly whites. It made me jump out of my skin, but the tail thumping on my leg and the lick that followed reasoned that all was well and I wasn't about to lose my nose!

It is important for you, the owner, to learn your dog's body language, which will indicate how he is feeling, and what response is expected. For instance, a dog lying in its bed that growls when approached is not being belligerent. It wants to be left alone, and is telling you so. And if you continue to approach you may be creating a problem that doesn't really exist – so simply leave him alone. 'Let sleeping dogs lie' – never a truer word said. Why he wants to be left alone is another matter entirely – tired, poorly, sore are the most common reasons.

It can be easy to misread our dogs in unique situations. Our hydrotherapy pool is a good example. Many owners believe their dogs are panicking in the water, when in fact they are relaxed and swimming well. Sometimes, even when the dog has got out wagged its tail, and run up the ramp again to get back in, the owners are still concerned that the dog is not happy. Only because they have come to the pool convinced that he would be scared! A dog reported as 'water phobic' – pulling to get into the pool room is another example. Trying to forget what we believe the dog should feel and watching its actual reactions, gives us a better idea.

4.7 Dog Talk

Dogs also communicate verbally, but in a much simpler way than we do. The alarm bark of a dog, which indicates the presence of potential danger, is one example. This bark tends to be loud, sharp and repeated quickly. Also, they have the ability to growl menacingly at something scary. An excited dog may give a high-pitched yip. Like with body language, you have to look at the situation and what is going on at the time. For instance, many dogs growl in play – it sounds scary, but the dog is just having fun.

Verbal communication coupled with body language can greatly increase the chance of us understanding our pets. For example, subtle whingeing and pacing with eye contact wavering between you and the kitchen could indicate the dog's restaurant should now be open, its well has dried up, or it needs a toilet break. Further investigation takes you into the kitchen, where the dog's next move will signal what he wants. Some dogs can be so unsubtle they simply plop an empty food bowl in your lap!

4.8 Using the Nose

Scent is another form of communication, one we thankfully do not get involved in. Can you imagine having to greet other people by butt sniffing? Scandalous! This is one trait that makes me glad I'm not a dog. Dogs sniff each other's bottoms, because there is information stored in the anal scent glands that indicates the animal's health, age, and sexual readiness. Almost without exception, dogs sniff each other whether they are meeting regular playmates or unfamiliar dogs. They will also lick at genital areas (the undercarriage!). This is perfectly normal, albeit a bit grim to us: certainly not something to reprimand the dog for – unless he is doing it excessively and irritating the other dog.

Both male and female dogs can use urine to make their mark. Dogs cock their back leg as high as they can, and some bitches' squat and raise a back leg in an attempt to squirt. Again it is dependent upon the individual breed and personality. The females that raise their legs are often more masculine in their general behaviour.

The world of scent is pretty alien to us. Our sense of smell is ridiculously poor when compared to animals and it is not a sense we rely on or use much. The smell has to be fairly strong for us to even notice it!

But for many of our dogs this sense is very important; for instance the cocker spaniel that walks with its nose glued to the floor, or the beagle that won't come when called and is zig zagging up the field. Sometimes we have to accept that our dogs are different and value things differently. A cocker won't train to walk as easily on the lead as a Labrador – it will value the smells on the floor higher than the treat in your hand and may need a harness to reduce the pulling and make the walk comfortable for both of you. A beagle may need a long line when in a field-type environment to help with recalls as the scent it picks up could take it far away.

A fun way to exercise your puppy's olfactory senses is to hide treats or toys around the house and garden for him to seek out and then eat or have fun with. To help him initially, try rubbing the treats on the ground or on plants to make a type of 'smelly pathway' for him to follow.

4.9 How Dogs Learn

Dogs learn in the same way that we do – by making connections between events. If an event has a good outcome, they are likely to repeat it, and if the result is not so good they are less likely to repeat it. This is often termed positive and negative reinforcement, but I prefer a less clinical and more descriptive approach – success and failure. Learning how to manage our dogs' successes and failures is dealt with in sections 4.12 and 4.14.

Dogs also learn by watching us and connecting events. For instance most dogs know when they are going out for a walk, way before we pick up the lead. The tell-tale signs are there in the clothes and shoes we put on. Equally they know when we are going out and they are not coming. I used to take my Heinz 57, Mutley, to college with me for lectures. He knew when it was lecture day because I would have a box file somewhere prominent in the house (typically by the front door so I would trip over it on my way out as I am quite forgetful). He would always be waiting by the door to go and the other dogs would all be in their spots with a 'didn't want to go anyway' look.

4.10 Success

Success makes you confident. The emotions behind success can be anything from mild amusement to euphoria, though the canine's idea of success may not be the same as ours. A dog successfully chasing off the postman each morning could well be in a state of euphoria. Raiding the bin can be successful sometimes and so can stealing from the kitchen – always worth a go, just in case the dog gets lucky. Pulling on the lead is successful - but only if you pull hard enough. This success gets the dog to that lamppost quicker and to the park in record time.

If a venture is successful to the dog, he will repeat it. When training our dogs we are always attempting to make the behaviour we like successful to the dog and the stuff we don't like, unsuccessful. Sometimes we are trying to make the behaviour we like *even more fruitful* than what the dog likes to do. Coming when called is a good example of this. Running around is fun, so we have to make coming back *even more* fun.

4.11 *Failure*

This is awful. Really failing at something can make you feel sad, depressed, insecure, and like you never, ever want to do it again. The depth of feeling associated with failure is often related to how much you wanted to succeed. But for our puppies and dogs we can help them to fail at the behaviour we don't like, and compensate it with success for the stuff we do like.

4.12 *Managing Success*

Ensure the activities that *you* like are successful for your dog. The emotional connection the dog makes guarantees they understand what we prefer and what will earn them something great. Signals of success include saying 'Clever boy (or girl)' in a happy manner, praising through stroking and cuddles, rustling a treat packet, or making a specific sound, like a click.

A clicker is a small, hand-held device that clicks when pressed. This sound is the same each time the clicker is used, and tells an animal when it has done something right (click means tick). The dog learns its significance by receiving a tasty food treat immediately after hearing the click. Often within three or four clicks and treats, the dog begins to look for the scoff on hearing the click. The click makes them feel successful, instantly. It then can be used as a marker – pin-pointing something they have done as very good. Dogs learn quickly with a clicker, as they know straight away what they have done to get their treat. Once they get into the clicker 'game', they do things to try and make you click. They stop watching your hand with the treats, and start focusing on the clicker hand. Offering you sits, downs, rollovers, and paws, they try their very hardest to make you click.

Their trying harder is an emotional element we can harness to teach them something new. Holding back on treats creates feelings of mild frustration in most dogs – but only when they know the treats are available. This frustration drives them to keep trying and trying, and if that fails – to try something else. For example, if you stand in front of a dog holding a food treat, it will show interest. Many dogs will sit, in the hopes that this will be enough. When the treat is not forthcoming, they might stand up and sit down again. This could be repeated several times until the dog eventually gives up, and tries something else – maybe lifting a paw. This could then be marked with a click, and a treat given. This is looked at again in Chapter Five with some interesting ways to train your puppy or dog in basic obedience.

It is important to understand that the clicker is for teaching new things – it helps speed up the learning process. Once the dog has 'got it' you don't need to use the clicker unless he gets lazy with tasks. So you don't need to carry the clicker with you when he's ten years old!

4.13 Motivating Your Dog

Any reward or treat on offer must be intensely gratifying to the dog. Some are motivated by the prospect of getting food, others by physical contact or the opportunity to hold or play with a particular toy. Many years ago, when my training school was in a converted vegetable patch in my back garden, I helped train a dog called Nemo. His one love in life was bread. You could offer him best steak, chicken, or top quality dog treats, and he'd turn his nose up in favour of stodgy white bread. But whichever prize is used with the clicker or success signal ('Good dog'), go on motivating your dog to learn. Keep the sweeties coming!

4.14 Managing Failure

A success signal for good behaviour should be balanced by equally clear-cut signals to show your dog he has failed to behave well. When a confident dog realises he's not going to get the treat he's hoping for, his mild frustration should spur him to try other ways of getting what he wants. However, if you punish him physically, his behaviour may become unpredictable. Your dog will learn better when he doesn't feel threatened and has 'options' regarding what to do next. This helps him to control his feelings and make an educated choice.

Many people signal bad behaviour using a firm 'No!' This should be said in a displeased tone, as initially it is all about the tone of voice. I could say to a puppy 'You're a nasty, smelly little beastie and I hate you' and he would stand and wag his tail at me as long as I said it in a nice voice. The tone is everything. Shouting does not really help in most cases as it can excite or frustrate many pups, making their behaviour worse. If the puppy doesn't stop behaving badly using a simple 'no' and a displeased look, then a time-out would be a good idea: two minutes away from the family to calm down. Pop him in the porch, downstairs toilet (removing access to chemicals and paper products!), his crate or outside, then allow him back in as though nothing has happened by opening the door, walking away and ignoring for 30 seconds so we don't reward the punishment.

Within two minutes, (or five to ten minutes if he's really crazy) you may want to consider what might be causing the puppy to misbehave. Is he bored? Hungry?

We do need to look at the puppy's day and ensure he is busy, rested, fed etc. at the times that fit in with your day.

For instance, if you like to watch TV in the evenings, ensure he is exercised and fed, then settle him down with a chew or give him a treat ball to play with so that you can enjoy your programme uninterrupted. It's no different than with children. If you wanted to do something and needed the children settled and busy, a children's DVD or two (like Disney) could be kept for such occasions.

It is important to note here that if we have told a puppy off for doing something we cannot then praise him for stopping as this is confusing and will encourage further bad behaviour. For instance, if you tell your pup 'no' for trying to steal your mobile and then when you get it off him you tell him he is a good boy, he will just hear good boy and *do it all over again*. The 30 second ignoring rule after any reprimand guards against this. By ignoring I mean no eye contact, no talking to or about said beastie and no touching.

Always keep calm with puppies and dogs. Getting all het up and irritable does not help anyone, least of all the puppy and you could end up making the situation much worse. Stay calm and be thoughtful as to what to do next remembering that whatever tactic you take, you need to take it for a period of approximately six weeks in order for it to work.

Chopping and changing your approaches to issues too frequently does not work.

Many people say to me in puppy classes (typically about toileting, play biting or stealing), that they have done everything they can to resolve the issue. All suggestions I then go on to make they have already done and it 'don't work'. I may have suggested three or four different approaches – all tried and failed already. But the puppy is only sixteen weeks old, so they haven't done anything for any length of time.

Consistent application is a must – puppies and dogs never change their behaviour overnight.

4.15 *Timing of Success and Failure*

A dog needs to make the connection between events – what he does and the outcome. For the link to be made the 'result' needs to happen either during the event, or immediately after, within two seconds. (This is where human learning is different, as we can make associations between events that have happened hours, days, or years previously).

When we are training a dog to sit, we need to signal success immediately he does so, as this is when he will be thinking about it. A few seconds later he could be thinking about something else, or doing something completely different. By using a success signal ('Good dog', click), we can mark the behaviour we approve of instantly, so there is no confusion. He knows exactly why he is being rewarded.

Failure is no different, except that if we are going to reprimand a puppy he *must* understand why – otherwise it's just random punishment, which could create mistrust. If you treated a dog at the wrong time there would be no serious repercussions. He would just assume you liked him – no problems there. If you reprimand at the wrong time there could be long-term associations for the dog. One of the most common examples of this is with house-training and chewing issues (see 3.22 to 3.24). If a dog toilets or chews something up when you are not there and you come back and tell him off, he is more likely to do it again. You then punish the toileting or chewing again, and a catch 22 situation begins. The dog becomes anxious on being left, expecting to be punished on your return. Toileting and chewing are common symptoms of anxiety. You then come home and fulfil his expectations by punishing him again. At no time will he connect your behaviour to his, because you didn't punish during the event. It could be thirty seconds to five hours later.

Timing of reprimands or punishment must be absolutely

spot on to avoid potential problems of misunderstanding.

4.16 *Being Consistent*

Using a consistent training system opens up a two-way communication process between our dogs and us (see Chapter Five). It is a method both parties can understand and stick to, while keeping the mutual bond strong. The earlier we give clear signals, for example the words 'no' or 'clever girl', the easier life can be. Always apply a method of altering behaviour (like stopping play biting) for six weeks. If the method hasn't worked by then, try something else. A confused dog will simply do its own thing.

4.17 *Practising Training*

While using something like a clicker greatly reduces the need for constant repetition, our dogs still need frequent practise. It is well known that dogs can modify their behaviour depending on the environment they are in. Training a dog or puppy once a week in class may produce an animal that is wonderfully behaved in that room, but it can act like a complete idiot walking down the street or off-lead in the park. Generally when training a dog you should teach it something in one place, perhaps at home, then practise in every place you might want it to 'perform'. This could be the street, the vets, a local park, or the mother-in-law's. Don't stop there – ask him to do the task regularly – so he doesn't forget! (see 5.1).

4.18 *Time-outs – For When the Puppy is Driving Us Crazy*

Sometimes telling a puppy off is not what is needed. There are those mad moments when puppies do 'the wall of death' around the living room, mowing down everything in their path. This is perfectly normal and is just blowing off steam.

All pups do this. You need do nothing but move your beer off the coffee table before it goes flying and sit back and enjoy the entertainment.

And then there's that silliness that comes from being over-tired, but not being able to 'give in', making them steal from under our noses, nibble our feet, and generally annoy us (see 2.3). This needs to be dealt with.

I ran puppy kindergarten for many years, and saw that our young pups are the same as little children when it comes to exciting situations. They give it their all, and then they get tired. But being so excited, they cannot switch off. Instead they continue, becoming more and more unbearable. Christmas and birthday parties immediately spring to mind! Towards the end of our kindergarten sessions, having had a good time running around and play fighting, the pups became grumpy or over-excited. This often led to scuffles and minor scraps. That's when they needed help to switch off and chill out.

The crate becomes invaluable at this time: a place the puppy can go where there is nothing but a chew-bone or small toy to play with. Switching the light off or placing a sheet over the top of the crate can encourage them to have a nap, so can playing classical music at low volume! It's no different to putting a child in their cot with a mobile (not a phone!), to encourage them to rest and calm down.

If there is no crate to hand, offering a tasty chew to a puppy on a comfortable cushion in the living room can be as good (although you may have to keep the room quiet). It helps the puppy to focus on one thing and cool off (as long as there is nothing going on to keep 'waking' the pup up again like people walking in and out). A bed in a utility room, or the kitchen is just as good.

If the puppy isn't tired and is just being a pain then use short two minute time-outs to help him learn to behave differently (see the end of 3.25).

4.19 Getting a Puppy Used to Wearing a Collar

Allow the puppy to become accustomed to the feel of the collar around his neck before clipping him onto a lead. Put the collar on your puppy and leave it on. To check it's comfortable, you should be able to slip two fingers easily into the collar. If it slips over the pup's head, tighten it slightly before using it with a lead. Your puppy may be sulky, sad, or continually scratching at his collar and shaking his head when he first wears it. The more it is left on, the quicker he will stop worrying about it. I personally recommend leaving them on permanently. The more fuss you make about the collar, (putting it on, rewarding him, taking it off again) the more fuss he will make about it. Check the collar fitting every few days – puppies grow very quickly.

In the UK, having a collar and tag on permanently and being microchipped is now a legal requirement for all dogs. The tag should have your contact details clearly written on it (your name and address including postcode is the minimum requirement). The ID tag is required even if your puppy has a microchip.

I also highly recommend the good old fashioned name tag as well, as many places do not have microchip readers, like your neighbour's house or the shop up the road. The tag comes into its own if your puppy goes missing locally. With your details clearly printed you can be reunited with your puppy within minutes. Microchips are only really useful if the tag comes off or is removed and it may take several hours / days / months to get your puppy back.

4.20 Teaching Your Puppy about His Lead

Pulling on the lead is rewarding, because it works. Dogs

are taught by us to pull. In the beginning they pull out in front, to get to somewhere that has caught their attention. We then pull them back. The dog tries harder to get where it wants, and increases his pulling. We pull back with all our strength. So it continues, until the lead going on becomes a signal for the dog to pull. A dog can be taught to pull on the lead in a few minutes, but it can take many months of mind-numbingly boring training to stop it.

Clip the lead onto your puppy when he is up and about and feeling lively. He may object to this and thrash around, or try and bite the lead. Encourage him to stop by putting a nice treat right under his nose. Take a step forward with the treat in your hand at the level of the pup's nose, and pop it in his mouth when he takes a step forward to join you. Most of us don't want our dog glued to our thigh when out walking, we just want him to be somewhere close to us, maybe slightly in front, or slightly behind. The important part is to keep the lead loose. When we think about success and failure, the success for the dog could be in getting you to walk faster. Failure is in not moving at all. Our success is to have the dog walking calmly at our side – so the more treats we use when we begin, the more likely we are to have a calm dog on a loose lead. Training classes are an excellent way of lead training.

Lead training can be frustrating once a dog has learned to pull. The excessive jerking on the lead may even hurt you. Do not be tempted, even in frustration, to pull back! In these cases it is better to resort to one of the many lead-training devices, such as head collars and harnesses, on the market. These do not train your dog to walk at your side, but they do reduce the pulling to give you the right set of circumstances to begin. Using one of these should not be deemed a failure. Some dogs naturally pull and this equipment is designed to help you and your dog have a pleasanter experience out walking (see 5.7).

4.21 *Make Food Fun*

The easiest way to keep dogs busy (whatever their age), is to look at feeding them differently. The food bowl is a purely human concept. We eat out of a bowl or from a plate, therefore so do our pets. It keeps the food in one place, is hygienic and easy to keep clean – all human values. However, with one of the main highlights of the day over in a couple of minutes, it leaves our dogs with few alternatives to satisfy their desire to seek out food, or keep them entertained. The desire for dogs to look for food is a true need, thwarted by life today.

Feeding time is looked forward to with great anticipation and eagerness. The desire to search for food can be a full-time occupation for some of our more 'greedy' companions. Just think how happy they would feel if feeding time really did last all day. We can actually make this happen in a way that works for our dogs and us. Dry food plays an important part in this. It not only ensures you feed a balanced diet, but is so versatile that each meal can be presented differently.

4.22 *Food-Dispensing Toys*

There are various ways we can make food more enjoyable. The first and most obvious are food-dispensing toys. They require the dog to work for its meal.

The dog moves the toy around with their paws and nothing happens. They then gets more inventive, and might 'bat' it with more force – still nothing. Out of extreme frustration they might pick it the toy up and drop it to the floor, or throw it. Bingo, some food escapes from the toy. Huge reward! The greater the frustration, the bigger the relief!

A Kong® is a conical shaped toy made of natural rubber which releases food relatively easily. Beginning with a basic Kong®, a dog can learn the principles of the food- dispenser.

Some dogs may find it difficult to solve a problem, which is effectively what they are doing when emptying a Kong®. Place a treat under a small, lightweight plastic cup. Make sure they see you do it. Then allow them to find their own way of getting the treat out. Once they have mastered this, they will find the Kong® easy.

Food-dispensing toys come in all shapes and sizes, and in a range of difficulty levels to keep the most intelligent dog busy. The Buster Cube®, due to its shape, is difficult to roll around. It also has a spiral device inside to ensure only a few pieces of food are released at a time. A Moleculeball® is a peculiar shape and only has one small hole at the top, again making it quite difficult. Then there's the Busy Buddy range – something for everyone there, and the Pyramids and Kong® Wobblers (weighted at the bottom so they keep springing back up – like Weebles). And don't forget all the varieties of treat balls, some complete with sound effects, for a more sci-fi experience.

Instead of placing treats in these toys, we could put in the dogs entire dry dinner, making them 'work' for each piece of their food. Hiding the toys around the house can complicate 'the hunt', encouraging them to use their nose and eyes.

4.23 Scavenging Problems

Dogs all have their own unique methods of emptying their Kong®. A Staffordshire bull terrier called Daisy learned very quickly at home that if she took the Kong® to the top of the stairs and dropped it, it would empty its contents as it bounced down. Some tend to push or knock the Kong® and then chase and capture it, often knocking morsels out as they do so. One particular youngster of the Heinz variety, an ardent scavenger called Sparkie, was so taken with the Kong® toy that he forgot his regular routine of hounding his owner when she was preparing dinner. Pleased with the prospect of preparing food without fending off the attentions of Sparkie, she began to fill his Kong® with tasty titbits every evening – an irritating problem solved simply and effectively.

4.24 Scattering Food

We can also feed our dogs like chickens. Scattering the food around the house or garden, we can send them off on a quest for food, to go out and seek each tiny bit, again encouraging them to use their eyes and noses. Sitting in front of the television, snuggled up and watching our favourite soap, we can entertain our pups by flicking their food around the room, satisfying their desire to chase and capture. Be inventive and ditch the dog bowl.

4.25 Making Our Dogs' Dinner Work for Us

By making dogs earn all of their food through training, we can keep them stimulated and mentally satisfied, with a superb side effect: they become 'trained' very quickly. This is a particularly nice way of feeding as we are not only keeping our dogs interested in performing tasks, but also making ourselves hugely rewarding to them in the process. The dog begins to see us as the source of all major 'goodies', strengthening the bond between us. Nervous or easily distracted dogs need this bond to be as strong as possible. It gives them the emotional anchor they badly need. I always highly recommend this method for new rescue dogs. It builds the trust quickly and the side effect is that the dog swiftly becomes trained.

4.26 Dogs that Gobble their Food

Eating too quickly causes indigestion. Indigestion causes bellyache and flatulence (bad smells). Some dogs eat so fast they vomit or cough and choke: not very pretty. Slow the eating down using the feeding methods above, or if you are food bowl fan, try a slow down bowl. This is a specially moulded bowl that has protruding parts in the bottom. As you put the food into the bowl, it falls between these protrusions. The dog has to eat around them, simply and effectively slowing down the eating. The Green Feeder is a good product to try for the super sonic eater.

4.27 Toy Rotation

A good variety of toys that can be easily changed will retain our pet's interest. If all toys are available, all the time, then their reward value drops. If toys are given in rotation, then the dog constantly gets 'new' toys to play with that hold their attention. Give two or three toys in the morning, and change for a different set later in the day to revive interest. Try for different toys the next day if possible.

Some 'parents' are concerned that their pup wrecks toys - but isn't that what they are there for? It's important to choose toys suitable for the dog's playing habits. Purchasing a cheap, latex, squeaky toy for an avid chewer is not a good idea, but a strong, sterilised bone stuffed with 'sweeties' is. There are some good variations now in the tough toy ranges with flavouring running down the middle of the bone (called Marrow Bone). My dogs love these and they are the only tough toys I have eventually had to replace – because they get so much use. Antlers (also called stag bars) and buffalo horns (also known as bullbars) are great as they don't splinter and dogs often chew them for hours at a time. They also last for weeks/months so even though they might seem a bit pricey a tasty antler / horn is a good investment.

When they are chewing their own toys, dogs are leaving our 'toys' alone. It's much cheaper in the long run to budget for new toys for the growing dog, than to replace the mobile phones and slippers he may have to resort to munching in the absence of anything else.

4.28 Games We Can Play

Games that we play with our dogs not only keep them happy, healthy, and stimulated, but also help them to see us as a source of interest and pleasure. Often they enjoy games that revolve around chasing and capturing. Naturally stimulated by small movements, a terrier can be fast asleep one minute, and hotfooting it after a squeaky ball the next.

4.29 Tug of War

One game that dogs adore is 'tuggy'. Sadly, this is a game we are advised not to play with our dogs as we are told that it encourages them to pit their strength directly against us, making them believe they rule the house. If we do play this game, we are told by some experts that we must win: we must never let go and allow the dog to control the toy. It makes the dog dominant over us (see 1.5 and 1.7). But having kicked this dominance theory into touch, we are free to enjoy this game, without feeling we are doing wrong or encouraging our dog to start paying the bills, gathering the food, and controlling the family.

I don't believe the dog is trying to win when playing tug. Winning is a human value. The dog is enjoying a game, which directly involves its 'parent', because when the dog is tugging furiously and you let go of the toy, your dog will almost certainly bring it back. He will try and place the toy in your hand, to entice you to play some more. Most of us do play this game, despite advice to the contrary, and it's often another whispered confession in a behaviour consultation. This is another area where we really need to trust our instincts.

4.30 Fetch

Fetch has no such superstitions attached. This excellent game is a favourite for many breeds of dog. It actively encourages chase and capture behaviour.

It can be a complex routine to teach a dog if it does not come naturally. Some dogs only do part of this game instinctively and have to be taught the rest. Herders tend to chase after a moving target, but may need encouragement to pick up the toy, then to bring it back, and finally to release it. Terriers nearly always 'kill' the toy, shaking it violently (and in the case of a ball on a rope, knocking themselves senseless in the process). Retrievers tend to find the bringing back part easy, but often don't want to let go. We should never pull items from our dog's mouths. This only encourages them to hold on tighter, and then we pull harder, they hold tighter and before we know it, it becomes a game of tug. Some may even feel threatened by this process, and become grumpy.

Lunging for the dog, to try and wrestle away the toy, increases the dogs' speed and agility. It becomes adept at out-manoeuvring us, and learns to tease instead of to bring back and release. (see 5.14 for how to teach fetch).

4.31 Teaching Fetch

Getting a dog to bring a toy back and release it is easier if you use two toys that are exactly the same. Throw the first one just a short distance from you, and allow time for the dog to pick it up. Once it is in the dog's mouth, call him to you. When he is near, bring the other toy out from behind your back and tease him with it. This makes him drop the first toy. Immediately throw the second toy as his reward. As he gets good at releasing the toy, begin saying 'leave'. Once he is leaving the article on this word alone, you no longer need the two toys. You can use treats, waving them under his nose to encourage him to release the toy, but we want the game to be self-sustaining. Using two toys does this for us. The toys have to be the same, or the dog will favour one over the other.

4.32 Getting Your Puppy to Drop Something

Please see 5.12 for teaching your puppy to leave from the beginning. If you need a quick fix, place a really tasty 'sweetie' right in front of the dog's nose, so he gets a good whiff of it. As he drops your slipper or iPhone, say 'leave it!' gently. Give him the treat and pick up the item at the same time, or your puppy might eat the biscuit and grab the article again.

This should not be used repeatedly as you run the risk of rewarding your puppy for grabbing articles in order to earn a treat. Teaching leave from the beginning is a better long-term strategy.

4.33 The Attention Seeking Thief

Most puppies will pick up things that are ours and explore them. The attention seeking thief will do this but will also always ensure we have seen them. Its then 'game on' as the pup scampers about the house and furniture hotly pursued by the irate owner. A tussle ensues as tempers are raised and the puppy is effectively taught that the only way to get really fun attention is by stealing. I have two poos (a cockapoo and a sproodle) and this behaviour is particularly rampant with these types of dogs. I have come to the conclusion that the only way of stopping this behaviour is to completely ignore it. It is different to the young puppy simply exploring our stuff. The whole point of the exercise to the puppy is to engage with us – the item stolen is not particularly important to them. By not engaging back the puppy will try harder to get our attention by stealing more things, parading up and down in front of us, chomping away at our prized possessions. And so he will try harder and harder, and then try something else.

With this issue, ignoring the dog completely, no eye contact or acknowledgement whilst going around the house and putting all valuables well and truly away is the only way forward. Leaving out things you don't care about so the puppy can steal and be ignored will then cure the issue. Paying lots of attention to your puppy when he has his own items and toys will speed the process up.

CHAPTER FIVE

Basic Training

5.1 How to Practise

I love dog training and taking classes – it is an absolute passion of mine. Seeing the light dawn in both species eyes as tasks start to come together is quite something to witness. And the relationship flourishes, as training a dog is all about opening up lines of communication between owner and dog. Learning to speak a bit of dog if you like as he learns a morsel of human!

One simple rule to follow is, *if he doesn't do, he doesn't get.* If you treat your puppy for not doing something, just because you love him and he looks dead cute, then he will learn really quickly that he needn't bother – the treat will come anyway. Dogs are smart like that.

Training should be fun. A game. And it is excellent for mental stimulation (and for tiring energetic dogs out that can't be walked for long periods as they are still growing or injured). The trick with training is not to be too regimental about it. It's easy for a dog to do a task if you are standing there in front of it, clicker at the ready, treats bulging out of your hand. They get the idea that you want them to do something. It's harder to get a dog just to respond to you whenever you need it to – so that's what we need to practise.

What I find works is doing a short training session, perhaps five minutes twice per day, to work on new things specifically. Then, start adding your training techniques into normal life. Having your treats tucked into a pocket perhaps ask your dog to sit and stay in the kitchen while you put the kettle on. Go back, reward him, then ask him to stay again while you put tea bags into the pot. Again go back and reward and maybe ask him to lie down. Tell him to stay while you pour the water etc.

Once you get onto tasks like out of sight stay perhaps use a similar technique. Instead of letting your dog just follow you into the kitchen while you grab a drink (a beer would be good!), tell him to stay. You may need to step out of the room and immediately go back in and work your way up the hall with frequent trips back, but he's learning to do an out of sight stay in a normal setting, not a training session. And you are earning your beer.

When all is said and done you need your dog to listen and respond in a normal family situation, so that's how I would recommend you to practise. It makes it more fun as well and not a chore to train the dog and you don't need to set aside any time to do it – so the age old excuse of 'I haven't had time' – just won't wash!!

5.2 How to Use a Clicker

You do not have to use a clicker to train a dog. Saying 'good boy (or girl)' followed by a treat can be just as good. But for those of you who want to try this method – here we go.

A clicker is a small hand-held device that makes a 'click' sound when pressed. We use it for training dogs as a marker, to tell the dog he has done something right. Basically click means tick! You've done something correctly. A treat or reward of some kind always follows the click, effectively telling the dog he's done it right AND a treat is coming. It makes training new tasks very quick and easy as the dog knows instantly when he has done something right and, more importantly, what he has done right. It makes it easy to get the dog then to repeat it. It is the immediacy and consistency of the click that makes it so effective.

Introducing a clicker couldn't be easier. Use a command the dog or puppy knows already – typically sit. Ask the pup to sit, click as he sits and then give the food reward. Repeat this four or five times and he'll have got it.

A clicker is a training aid – it helps dogs to learn quickly. It is not one click for yes and two clicks for no. It is a simple click as the dog performs a task correctly, followed by a reward. Once the dog has achieved the task and is performing reliably, then you don't need to use the clicker (I know this is a concern of many people that if they use a clicker, they will always have to use it). If he gets lazy with the task, have a quick refresher using the clicker. You shouldn't be using the clicker for a sit when the dog is ten years old!

5.3 Name

This is a repeat of section 2.1. Teaching your puppy its name is first in a long line of things they need to learn, and choosing the name is the first step. Two-syllable names are the easiest for our pets to grasp – for example Tosca, Mutley, Homer and Sadie. Long names are nice but may need shortening for everyday use.

Most puppies learn their names quickly without us really having to do any specific training for it. Just using it while paying the puppy attention is often enough.

If not, try this. Call your pup's name in a cheerful and excited voice, while it is quite close to you. If it looks around or comes to you, show you are happy by stroking it, giving it a food treat or offering a game of something it likes. Try not to over-use the name, as your pup may learn to ignore it. Only call him if you want him for something nice. Being called and then told off is a very quick method of teaching your dog its name is not a pleasant thing to hear.

5.4 Sit

A quick method to teach a young puppy to sit is to hold the food bowl over his head at dinnertime and wait. As soon as he sits down (often in frustration) say 'sit' and give him his dinner.

You can also teach this using a food treat. This method is a bit more versatile and not restricted to feeding time. Hold the treat over the pup's head, taking it just over the eye line very slowly. As the pup looks up and the treat starts to disappear over his head, he sits. There is no need to push down on the back end at all and in fact forcibly making a dog sit can make the whole process take longer as the dog instinctively pushes back.

You say 'sit' as the dog sits. Try saying it just the once as repeating it could make the signal 'sit sit sit' and the dog does not understand to respond to just 'sit'. The hand with the treat in it is also serving as a hand signal and a dog will learn this visual signal faster than the word. (A combination of hand signals and words is always the fastest way to get reliability). The hand signal I always stick to is just as if I have a treat in my hand and am holding it out in front of the pup (my thumb, first finger and middle finger pressed together, palm upwards).

Practise the sit at kerbs, for having the lead on, for giving a chew or a special toy making this a pre-requisite for anything the dog might get. This way they catch on quick.

Quick Overview

1. Stand in front of your puppy. Engage his attention on the treat in your hand by showing him it or waving it around his nose. Hold the treat slightly above his head

going *slowly* over his eye line (towards his back).
2. As he follows the sight of the treat his bottom plops down. Say 'sit' once, click, then give the treat.

5.5 Down

Down is the next progression. Sit or kneel on the floor. Ask your puppy to sit, don't treat it (as it might think it's finished and get up and walk away). Hold a handful of tasty bits up to the pup's nose – try and connect the nose to your hand by allowing the puppy to sniff and nibble. Slowly, keeping the nose connected this way take your hand down to the floor and pull it slightly forwards. Hold your hand there; this is a time for patience. As soon as the puppy flops down say 'down' once (don't shout or say it loudly, a puppy's hearing is usually excellent). Give the treat. If using a clicker, you would click as soon as the pup is down, say 'down', and then give the treat. Repeat this straight away starting from the sit again.

If you have tried this multiple times and he keeps standing up try going slower with your hand movement and keeping it closer to your pup's chest. If this doesn't work sit down on the floor with your legs out in front of you. Make a slight bridge by raising your knees off the ground (creating a tunnel). Encourage your dog under the tunnel by teasing him with your handful of treats. As long as your knees are at the right height your puppy will follow the treats into the tunnel and automatically lie down. Click, say 'down' and give one treat. Repeat a few times and then go back to doing it from the sit position as above.

It is worth noting here that some dogs get this exercise straight away while some need a little time and can take a few sessions to grasp what is needed to earn the treat. Don't be tempted to push down on the dog's back or to pull his front legs out from underneath him so he crashes to the floor (and don't let anyone else do it either). These are old fashioned methods in the worst case could cause physical harm, and at best case could make your dog unhappy about doing downs.

Once your pup has done this five to ten times it is worth progressing it on straight away. After all you don't want to have to grovel on the floor with your dog when he is six years old to get him to lie down. What we want is to be able to stand up, point to the floor and say 'down'. Getting there quickly is a good objective.

Now you want to be standing up and bending over instead of sitting or kneeling down. Holding several treats in your hand make a point with your index finger (like shooting with a pretend gun). Bend over and glue the dog's nose to your hand as above. Go down most of the way stopping about two to three centimetres off the ground and hold that position while saying 'down' at the same time. Your dog should flop straight down. If he doesn't, stay where you are and don't be tempted to go all the way to the floor.

Thinking time for the puppy is needed, as the signals you are giving are slightly different. Stay there and only start again if your puppy gets up and walks away. If your puppy is finding this change difficult, take your hand down slower. Don't keep stopping and starting, pointing to the floor and repeating down. This just creates confusion and the dog's head just bobs up and down. Clear, slow, consistent signals are what we are aiming for. Don't forget to click and treat. You can repeat the down word if you can't help yourself: but you don't have to if you said it as the dog went down.

The next time you do down, (straight away would be good), hold your hand just a little higher – and so on and so forth – until you are standing and pointing to the floor. This process can be done in a few minutes but can also take several days / weeks of short training sessions.

Now start adding down into your daily life and perhaps transpose some of the situations you would normally ask for a sit, to a down.

Quick Overview

1. Start in the sit position.
2. Using a handful of treats engage his attention on your hand by showing him them or waving them around his nose.
3. Slowly take your hand down to the floor, vertically, keeping his nose interested.
4. If he is not lying down yet, *slowly* pull your hand away from him along the floor.
5. As he flops down, say 'down' once.
6. Click and give one of the treats.

5.6 Stand

Stand is one of the easiest tasks to train for and also the one you are least likely to use. Typically stand is used when grooming a dog or when at the vets checking limbs and joints. But it is useful to know, particularly for the veterinary situation where the dog can already be under some emotional pressure and pulling it around to force it to stand up can increase the stress.

Start in the sit position (that's the dog, not you). Hold a treat to the pup's nose and pull it forward, horizontally in line with the dogs nose and, very slowly. As the dog follows the treat, it automatically stands. Click, say stand and give the treat. Make sure you don't pull the treat upwards at all – as this is the sit signal and will cause confusion.

Some pups will bum-shuffle along the floor or lie down. Don't stop. Keep pulling the treat slowly (and horizontally) forwards. After a few seconds of cleaning the floor with its bottom, or crawling along on its belly, the dog will stand. If you do stop and start again you will have to go through the whole bum-shuffling sequence again.

The hand signal for stand can then be introduced once you have repeated it a few times. Hold a treat between your index and middle finger. Keep your palm flat and palm side towards the dog (engaging the nose with the treat). Slowly pull forward and say stand. As he stands, click and give the treat. Your hand signal then becomes a flat palm pulled away from the dog. Simple!

Quick Overview

1. Start with your dog in the sit position.
2. Hold a handful of treats up to his nose.
3. *Slowly*, pull your hand horizontally away from your dog in line with his nose.
4. As he stands, say 'Stand' once.
5. Click and then give one of the treats.

5.7 Walking on a Loose Lead

This objective should be taken as a work in progress with young dogs (and some older dogs!!) and requires persistence, consistency and oodles of patience. Dogs like to get where they are going quickly, especially if it's the park. Putting a lead on stops them from going at the pace they want to, so they pull against it. We automatically pull back, they pull harder and hey presto we have successfully taught our dog to pull on the lead.

Try and think differently about the lead. See it as a safety chord, rope or chain, not as something we use to control the dog. The lead is there to stop the dog running off and doing something stupid. You control the dog using food, treats, a toy – just encouraging him to follow you and creating *the habit* of following you. Sounds simple – but simple it is not!

I am right-handed so I'm going to explain this for the right-handed person. If you are left-handed or have a weakness on one side then walk the dog on whichever side is more comfortable for you.

Holding the lead in your left hand. KEEP YOUR LEFT ARM RELAXED (shake it out if you need to). Shorten the lead so the dog can only take one step away from you maximum. We don't want to give him too many options, because he'll take them. Put the clicker in your lead hand if you are using one. Have a treat bag on (or bum bag, similar to a treat bag but clips around your waist) so you can get at your treats easily. Have a handful of treats in your right hand and hold this hand across your body so it sticks out just above your left hip. Engage the dog's nose with the treats and if needed waggle your hand about as you move forwards *at a normal pace*. (Try and walk at a regular speed. I don't know why but many people walk at snails pace when doing heel and this is very boring for a dog).

After two or three steps click, say heel and treat. Repeat this a few times and once your dog starts to get the idea click, say heel and treat perhaps every five or six paces. Once this is starting to get some consistency say 'heel' and click every eight or nine paces but perhaps only treat every two or three clicks. Otherwise you can get through a bag of treats just getting up the drive.

As your dog becomes competent at this reduce the clicks and treats. This can take many weeks / months.

If your dog pulls, stop dead. If your arm is rigid and tense you will tolerate a huge amount of pulling, so make sure it is relaxed. It can then act as a barometer and as soon as your arm goes up past 90 degrees stop dead. Engage the nose again and perhaps take two to three steps backwards bringing the dog back into your side. Then start again. This is where the frustration kicks in for both dog and owner as you repeat ad nauseum (until you want to scream).

Try and stay calm and relaxed.

It is very important that your lead arm is relaxed and down at your side in a normal position so you know when to stop dead. By stepping two to three paces back your whole body then takes the strain of bringing the dog back at your side – not just your arm. This allows anyone of any build to use this method, not just body builders!. Adding a sit after you have stopped can help to calm an over excited dog.

Practise heel in the garden and around the house (or in any secure area) without using a lead but following all the steps above as if a lead is attached. This is the best way to practise walking on a loose lead. Then you just add the lead in after.

For dogs that have learned to pull on the lead it is often necessary to use a training aid such as a head collar or harness. Please do not view this as a failure on your part or that your dog is faulty in some way. Most young dogs pull. They are simply excited and eager. These training aids take the pull out of the dog giving you the right circumstances to then train him as above. It is difficult in the extreme to lead-train a dog that is fighting against you all the way, but it can give you Popeye muscles if you are partial to that look! It's not forever either. I advise many people to walk the dog out on an aid of some description and once it has had a run around walk back on his collar. This can work well as a compromise. And for us women, with limited upper body strength, it can make the difference between us walking the dog or not walking him (or grabbing every lamp post on the way to the park to reduce our speed!)

And sticking a choke (codename check) chain, noose (codename slip lead), pinch or prong (sticking spikes into your dogs neck) collar or any other such instrument of torture on the dog is completely unnecessary and rather cruel.

As for which kit to use, that is a tricky question. One method of determining what to go for is if the dog is pulling all the time, go for a head collar (like a Gentle Leader). If he is pulling some of the time, then try a harness. The harness should be one where the lead clips onto a ring at the dogs chest which corrects pulling (like an Easy Walk), not a basic body harness (clips on in the middle of the back) as these encourage the dog to pull harder and may cause muscle loss on the back legs as the front end builds to almost Staffie proportions. Obviously if the dog *really* objects to a head collar (they all object a bit), then go straight to a pull correcting harness.

Whichever kit you choose it should ultimately fit easily, be comfortable for the dog (not cause chafing etc) and make walking easier and more enjoyable for both of you. You may have to try a range of walking aids before you find what is right for you and your dog.

If you think about it in terms how a dog is built and the relative delicateness of the neck area, a collar is possibly the worst place to try and control the beastie. Long term you could be looking at neck damage, muscle build-up in all the wrong places and throat problems. Any of these can occur if the dog is constantly pulling on a collar: and if he's coughing or gagging while walking, change to a correcting device straight away.

Quick Overview

1. Hold the lead in your hand that is next to the dog. Put the clicker in this hand (if using one). Keep your lead arm relaxed.
2. In your other hand have some nice smelly treats.
3. Hold your treat hand across your body so it sits by your

waist or just above your hip.

4. Wiggle your treat hand to get your dogs attention.
5. Start walking at normal pace.
6. Click if he is following your hand, say 'heel', and release a treat.
7. Aim to increase the number of steps between each click and treat.
8. Alternatively, don't reward each click. Try every two or three clicks for every treat and keep expanding this.
9. If your lead arm goes above 90 degrees stop dead, take three paces back to bring dog back in at your side, and continue walking. No good dog, no click!
10. Alternatively, don't reward each click. Try every two or three clicks for every treat and keep expanding this.

5.8 Coming When Called

Dogs need to learn to come when called (commonly referred to as recall) in a variety of situations, for example at the end of a walk. They have to be called away from other dogs or people they find interesting, just as they have to be called in from the garden, or after escaping out of the front door after a cat. Teaching the dog to come when called is one of the main reasons people attend training classes.

Ideally the training should begin with your puppy around the house and garden before he's even allowed out. Letting a puppy off the lead in a field or park at twelve to fourteen weeks (as soon as they have had their vaccinations) is a scary prospect – but in fact it's the best time. They are very dependent upon you just now. Waiting until the puppy is six months old, a teenager, knowing where he is and how to get home, reduces the likelihood he will return to you, or even care where you are. If a dog of any age has a problem returning when called, then you'll need to re-train from scratch.

Firstly we want them to respond quickly to the sound of their name. This can be achieved by calling the dog's name when he is nearby, and rewarding him with praise or a treat when he looks round at you. The name is the attention getter! Then we have to teach them another word that means 'come back'. Words like 'come' are poor – dogs always respond better to two syllables, like 'come here'. ('Here!' is the signal I use, but I pronounce it 'hee-yah'.) In the house, walk past your dog and call him – 'Cricket, come here!' – keep *walking away* from him. Offer big praise, a food treat, or a quick game the instant he catches up with you. If you're using a clicker, this is the time to click, and then give a 'sweetie' (see 4.12 and 5.2). Do this off and on throughout the day, around the house and garden. (Repeating this over and over will often bore a dog – try not to overdo it).

If you call your dog and stand still he may look, decide he knows where you are and continue what he is doing. If you call your dog, and then walk towards it, you are undoing your training and the dog reads the situation as he hears the command. This can lead to a lovely game of chase. Lovely for the dog, not for us!

Once a dog starts coming when you call him (which could take a few minutes, hours or days), we need to change the number of times we give him a sweetie for doing it. Dogs like to gamble. A dog can make a decision as we pay witness to each day, 'Shall I steal the steak off the kitchen table?' he wonders, nose twitching and scanning for goodies. He decides quickly, depending on the value of the prize and how easy it is to steal. Even dogs previously caught pilfering will check where we are and do a swift risk-assessment.

The basic factors in their decision-making are 'where's the loot?' and 'what risk is there in getting it?'

This is no different to the dog who hears his owner calling him, weighs up his options, turns tail, and runs off in the opposite direction. Some even look back as if to say 'not yet!' The poor owner is left stranded, with no option but to shout, stamp his feet, wave his lead in the air and blow on his whistle. All good frustration outlets, but they don't get the dog back. Telling the dog off when he finally does return can reduce your frustration, making you feel temporarily better. But all it teaches the dog is that 'come here' really means 'come here and be punished!' ensuring the dog is even more reluctant to come back next time.

What we need to do is stack the odds in our favour. Make the choice easy. We hold the reward, and it is one worth having, but it is only available if the dog returns quickly. However, giving a reward every time a dog comes back to us starts it thinking. 'Do I want the biscuit, or shall I go and sniff in those bushes?' It's better to mix rewards with praise – we should always be happy to see them – and perhaps offer some dog food for a reasonable return, but give them a very special treat for turning on a sixpence and racing towards the owner at full speed (remembering to put the brakes on, of course).

The special 'come here' treat must be something the dog prizes above everything else. It needs to be changed frequently, to keep the dog really interested. Showing the dog the reward before you allow him offlead hones his senses as to what he could earn. Dogs understand the rules of a game swiftly, and the 'come here' game can be taught in a couple of sessions in the garden or on an extender lead, using a multitude of rewards with a differing range of values. With some, a squeaky toy can be that highly regarded prize.

5.9 Coming Back Issues

Problems with coming back are numerous. Some dogs go completely deaf momentarily, while others can glance in your direction acknowledging they have heard, but still refuse to return. The teasing types come in close, and then dart just out of reach. These have often learned to do this through being grabbed. Hunting dogs become so involved in the eye, stalk, chase, pounce, bite, kill routine that nothing else matters once they have caught a scent. The desire to be chased spurs some dogs on. As you take a step towards them, they run off. These dogs have often been taught this in the back garden – you chasing your dog for fun – and then transpose the game to the field. Playing with other dogs can be great, while returning to you may be a bit boring. The dog is only called in at the end of the walk may decide it's not yet time. When being trained to 'come here' using food, some dogs quickly learn to grab the grub, and then scoot off – very clever and doubly rewarding. The stubborn amongst them may just stay where they are, and insist you go and fetch them!

Starting 'come here' from the beginning and keeping them on an extender lead or long line in the meantime is a sensible way forward. Each time your dog ignores you when you call him, the pleasure of being free motivates him to do it again. Dogs who take the food and run need to be taught that they only get the food once the lead is on or you have hold of their collar. This can be quickly achieved by holding the food tightly in your hand, allowing the dog to sniff and lick at it, and releasing it slowly. While the dog is concentrating on the food hand, slip the other hand through the collar. Once you have a good grip of the collar then release the rest of the food. Keep hold of the dog and make a fuss of him. Ask him to sit. Once he has sat tell him to 'Go play'. At this point let go of the collar. Many dogs see the lead being unclipped as a sign to run off, but if you always get the dog to sit, hold his collar, and then tell him to 'Go play', the dog learns that he cannot go until you say so. This avoids the problem of having to fight with the dog to get the lead off.

5.10 Hide and Seek

This is a great game to play with your dog on walks. As he is sniffing at a tree or burying his nose in a bush, vanish quietly behind something and keep silent. (You must keep very quiet or your dog will suss out where you are using his ears and may not feel the need to seek you out). Wait for him to come and find you. When he does find you, throw a party – give him a sweetie and loads of fuss. This game makes your dog use his nose to find you, something dogs like to do. It also teaches him to keep an eye on where you are – to continually check you are still around.

5.11 Stopping Jumping Up

It's true that little puppies are cute and people tend to encourage them to jump up. But they grow, and some grow very quickly and can begin to hurt people quite early on. So, this behaviour does need to be nipped in the bud quickly, ideally when the dog is a puppy or adolescent, before a real habit is formed.

Dogs jump up at people to get attention and it usually works. Even if that attention is 'ouch', or 'Buster stop' screamed loudly while the dog is pushed off. There are several methods that I find work well for this problem and a combination of them used in different situations can quickly stop this from becoming a major issue quickly.

When meeting people out in the street or visitors to your house: Immediately your puppy goes to jump up at them pull back on the lead, harness or collar and say 'No, get off'. Then give your sit command. When sitting (or standing) slip your fingers into his collar or harness and apply slight downward pressure so your dog can then be fussed by the person he was trying to jump on without the risk of him jumping up and head butting. If he goes to jump up again, pull back, say

'No, get off' and then 'sit'. (Don't be tempted to give treats for this or tell your dog it is good as your dog will learn to jump up, in order to be told to get off, and then sit for a treat). The reward for behaving nicely is the attention from the person he wants it from i.e. the visitor. Be consistent with this – no attention unless sitting – and your dog will quickly give up jumping at people.

When your dog jumps up at you or other household members because you have been out for a while and the dog is over-excited, a different approach may work better. There are a few options for this. Choose whichever suits you best and apply it for six weeks to two months consistently.

> ***Option 1.*** Ignore your dog when you get home. Your dog is looking for attention, which is fine. It's just the method he is employing that is annoying. Ignore him completely (don't look at him, talk to him, touch him) so the jumping up strategy does not work in getting the dog what he wants. Eventually he should stop and look to other ways to say hello. The downside to this method is that he will try harder so you do have to be prepared to go through an escalation of the jumping (maybe a little nipping or clothes grabbing) for him to finally give it up and try something else. This escalation could take hours, days, weeks, months – depending on how sure the dog is in his own mind that jumping up is the way to go. You just have to be prepared to go through that. This works well for some people.

Another downside to this method is that your dog may be very sensitive and feel he is in trouble or that you are upset with him as you are ignoring him. This can in some cases cause some anxiety in the dog and he may pee or poo when he is left, or start chewing things he never has before. If you see these side effects, stop this method immediately.

Option 2. An alternative to this is asking for a simple sit. Keep a treat or special toy in your pocket or in the porch. As you walk through the door say a calm 'hello' and give your hand signal and word for sit (see 5.4). Wait patiently, maybe waving the treat around gently to focus his attention on it. Once he sits, maybe then ask for a down (hand signal plus word see 5.5). Give the treat and a calm stroke and he should be calm enough not to jump. Sit and down are often used by trainers and behaviourists as a calming down position. Try this method for six weeks to two months – he should come and sit automatically after this time if everyone does the same. (If the dog is still jumping up at one or two individuals and not at the rest of the household then their consistency should be improved).

Option 3. Another fun way of stopping this type of jumping up is to keep a nice toy (perhaps a squeaky) in the porch or on the doorstep. As you walk through the door give it a couple of squeaks and then throw it. Many dogs will go after the toy and then trot around with it wagging furiously. If the dog catches on to this one he may then automatically go and grab a toy when you come through the door. Simple, easy and very little effort needed. There are no downsides to this approach that I have found to date – other than with the dog that doesn't value toys!

Option 4. Do ballroom dancing. Without looking at the dog step away so he falls to the floor. Keep calm and relaxed. As he comes from the right side, step left. As he comes from the front, step back etc. This is a very calm, passive approach and the dog simply keeps falling to the floor and gains no attention whatsoever. I love this method as it is stress free for all and does feel like ballroom dancing!

For the dog that starts jumping up (and possibly nipping or grabbing at clothing) at random we need to be quite firm. The randomness of this is what causes most difficulties as a dog can easily catch you off balance and knock you over – he doesn't need to be particularly big. Yes, he wants attention but we really shouldn't give him any for this – he will never stop otherwise. I find a time-out works really well (see 4.18). Simply get hold of his collar and carry or walk him to the porch or to the back door and put him out of the way for two minutes. You don't usually need longer than this, but if he comes back in all lairy do it for a bit longer. It's a calm-down session for him and is quite a strong punishment as he is being excluded from the family. Don't shout or get angry – say nothing. Just eject him quickly. When he is allowed out again ignore him for 30 seconds and then act as though nothing has happened. If he starts his crazy behaviour again, repeat this process. Consistency in this approach should stop this behaviour in a few weeks. Don't forget to ignore him for 30 seconds when you open the door so you don't reward him by mistake.

5.12 Teaching Your Puppy to Leave

Getting a dog of any age to leave is very important. And I'm not just talking about getting him to drop your new iPhone either. There are many things around the house, garden and especially out on walks that will attract a puppy or adult dog that could be potentially harmful, even deadly. Teaching leave in a harsh way by yanking items off them or physically pulling the dog away can encourage the dog to run away from you or worse still, swallow what they have or beome aggressive. Leave needs to be taught properly and gently in order for it to have the long-term benefits you can achieve.

You can start this, as with any training, at any age. But it is always easier if you do it sooner rather than later.

Take two handfuls of the puppy's or dog's food. Kneel down on the floor. Don't give the dog any command like sit or down. Place a piece of food on the floor and say 'leave it' gently. (You can use leave, but the two syllables in 'leave it' tends to give a quicker and stronger response). As the dog goes for the food, push him away (non-aggressively) using the same hand and as you do pop a piece of food in his mouth. I find that pushing the food into his mouth works best, so you are basically pushing against his muzzle. Immediately put another piece of food on the floor again saying 'leave it' and push away using the food and popping one piece in his mouth. Continue with this (reloading from your other hand) until all the food is gone. Pick up the pile on the floor and start again.

Of course we want all this to be gentle and nice, but it may be a bit of a scramble in the beginning and you might have to fend off the beast using the other arm as a block for the first few goes. Don't get harsh, or be tempted to get cross. Then only reward for this and push back giving no treat if he comes forward when you put food down and say 'leave it'. Then two or three bits down to every one the dog gets (increasing all the while until you can dump a pile of food on the floor and give just one piece in reward for leaving it).

Once you can do this easily (and it might take a few meals given like this over a week) then we are ready to move on.

Take something tasty, like a pig's ear or juicy bone and place it on the floor. Put your dog's lead on – very important. Walk him up to the item keeping the lead shortish so he can't just make a grab for the treat. Hold him there, about ten centimetres away. Don't yank on the lead or let him touch or lick the item. Gently say 'leave it' repeatedly until he turns away from the tasty item. Immediately click or say 'good dog' but about three metres away and walk him away so he learns to leave and come right away from something. Walk him up and repeat what you have just done, remembering not to yank at all on the lead. Only repeat this once or twice. You are now ready to take this exercise out on your walks.

Practising leave on walks is really important. This is the time you need this the most and there are always plenty of things to practise with. As you are walking up the street or in the park and your dog shows interest in some rubbish, a poo, etc., hold him there like you did at home and repeat 'leave it' to him, remembering not to shout or to yank on the lead. Praise when he finally comes away voluntarily, walk away and reward eight plus metres away.

The reasons for not shouting I have already given, but why not a yank down the lead – surely he will learn quicker?

Yes, your dog will learn more swiftly, but it is dependent upon him being on the lead. A dog doesn't really need to learn leave on the lead as we can always just pull him away. What we want is for him to learn to leave stuff when he is *off the lead*, so we cannot use the lead as part of the signalling process. It must be entirely voluntary from the dog. This is crucial in terms of getting a decent leave from a loose dog.

With this exercise the more practice you do out on your walks, the more proficient he will get and if he gets bored of it – great! He will stop going for stuff, which is what we want in the long run. Don't set him up with items at home – you'll be wasting your time as dogs catch on quick that they can't have it, so learn nothing new, or they learn to go for it in order to be told to leave it to earn a treat which is not what we are looking for. If you only practise this on your walks with real life rubbish, which is different and in a different place each time the side effect is learning to ignore stuff – the ideal outcome.

Quick Overview

1. Have food in both hands. Put a piece down and with the same hand push the dog away and pop food in his mouth. Repeat until the dog doesn't move forward when you put the food down. Then you only reward that.
2. If the dog comes forward when you put the food down after this gently push away with no food. Only reward for putting it on the floor and the dog not making moves.
3. Repeat until you can put lots of food down saying 'leave it' each time you do.
4. Take your practise out on a walk. For every unsavoury item he expresses interest in, stand still, repeat 'leave it' in a happy voice until he voluntarily comes away, walk away praising and treat eight ish metres away.

5.13 Stay

Stay means 'do nothing while I go away and come back'. That's what we want the dog or puppy to learn. This exercise is very useful.

To begin with simply ask your dog to sit in front of you. Don't reward the sit. Then try and turn around on the spot in front of him. If he is still sitting click and give him a treat. If not, try again. If he really won't sit for a full turn, try a half turn remembering to take your face away, and build it up to a full turn. Once you have mastered the full turn add in the word 'Stay'. Using a flat hand for your hand signal (almost like you are going to pat him on the head, without being that close). Give the hand signal and word at the same time and turn around on the spot again. Once you have done this a few times, remembering to reward each time, then start turning and taking one step away.

Ask your dog to sit using the word and hand signal. Then stay, again using the word and hand signal. Turn your back on him and take one step away as normally as possible (don't start walking funny and acting all stiff as this can unsettle the dog). Turn back to him and step back. Click or say 'good dog' and reward him straight away. Repeat this and try and add in an extra step away each time if you can, without him getting up to follow you. If he does start getting up you may have to do three steps away several times until he's got it then move on to four steps. Then all you need to do is gradually increase the time and distance away.

There are four rules to stick to in order for your stay to be reliable.

1. Never call his name while you are away from him. If you want to remind him to stay, just say 'stay'. Saying 'Max stay' may induce him to come to you. Some people think the dog should be looking at them when doing a stay and call the name to get the attention, swiftly undoing all their hard work. Personally I am happy if the dog is looking around, as long as he is staying. (Thumb up bum and brain in neutral is what we really want – that indicates a nice relaxed stay, which can then be used in daily life).

2. Never call him to you – always go back and reward him for staying put. If you start calling him to you, the stay will become unreliable, as the dog will interpret the slightest signal from you to be 'come'. Scratching your nose for example, or raising an eyebrow could set the dog off on a mad scramble to come and get the treat, and this is definitely not a relaxed calm stay. Always, always, always go back, stand in front of him and then click or say 'good dog' and reward.

3. Don't be tempted to walk backwards. Your dog has to learn to behave in a stay even if your back is to him (which is why we do the turning around bit at the beginning). If your dog can only stay put while you are facing him – then he can't do a stay. Let's face it – teaching him by walking backwards doesn't really give you a usable task unless you go round walking backwards in your regular life. And you might just fall over something...

4. If your dog sits up, lies down or stands up while doing a stay, but does not move off the spot you can still reward him. Simply put him back into the original position first and then click or say 'good dog' and treat.

Practising stay can be boring for a dog. Vary where you practise and what you are doing as you walk away: maybe putting the kettle on, getting the dog a treat out of the cupboard etc. Only do a handful of stays several times a day, some in the kitchen, some in the garden, some out on walks,each day as or your dog might get bored or frustrated and not want to play that game.

5.14 Fetch

Getting a dog to bring a toy back and release it is easier if you use two toys that are exactly the same. Throw the first one just a short distance from you, and allow time for the dog to pick it up. Once it is in the dog's mouth, call him to you. When he is near, bring the other toy out from behind your back and tease him with it. This makes him drop the first toy. Immediately throw the second toy as his reward. As he gets good at releasing the toy, begin saying 'drop'.

Once he is leaving the article on this word alone, you no longer need the two toys. You can use treats, waving them under his nose to encourage him to release the toy, but we want the game to be self-sustaining. As you are essentially rewarding him for dropping the dog starts dropping earlier and earlier and not bringing it back to you so using two toys achieves this for us The toys have to be the same, or the dog will favour one over the other.

5.15 Wait

Once you have a reliable stay and your dog has been performing this in many different places you can start with wait. (You need a good, solid stay before you start working on this one, or you may lose your stay - so be patient).

Wait should be thought of as a pause, followed by another task. The most common use of wait is when it is followed by 'come here'. For instance, asking your dog to sit and wait at the front door, you step through, and then call your dog through. Wait has many, many applications on and off the lead, and is well worth training for.

Start with a sit at the side of you. Give the stay hand signal, but use the word 'wait' instead of 'stay'. Take two steps forward and then call your dog in to the side of you and into sit. Click or say 'good dog' and reward. Increase the distance between you each time by one or two steps. Then you can start using wait. Use it at kerbs, asking your dog to sit and wait, then come as you cross the road. Getting out of the car – open the boot or door immediately giving the hand signal and the word 'wait', then call him out of the car. Using wait at doors in and out of the house gets this exciting situation under some control. Off-lead in the park you may be coming up to a corner, give the signal 'wait' as you check all is good, then perhaps something like 'on you go', to say he can move again.

Wait is simply a pause, followed by another command, and for this reason it is one that can be practised a lot in many different situations without the dog getting too bored.

CHAPTER SIX

Six to Eighteen Months (ish)

6.1 Living with Teenagers

Suddenly your charming, sweet and adorable puppy turns into a teenager. Hormones raging, their behaviour can at this age become hugely irritating. All those hours put into teaching them how to behave, and they stick up two fingers and do their own thing anyway. We know all about teenagers – we were those spot-infested creatures once! Most dogs do not get spots but they do get other annoying traits. Teenagers grow up, and most of our dogs will be at their worst for just a few weeks – so do not despair. Many owners say that puberty is the hardest time they had with their puppy and it strikes suddenly – they kind of wake up like it one day!

By sticking to our house rules (see 3.10), and using clear and consistent signals for good and bad behaviour (see 4.12 and 4.14), we can get through this phase and come out the other end with our relationship stronger than ever before. But if we confront, pick fights over small issues, and get all het up about things, we may despair and so may they. Many dogs in this age group are brought to me for behaviour problems, when in fact they are just being awkward due to their age. Some are even rehomed via rescue centres during this period – in fact many, many dogs are put down or rehoused in this life stage – but what we need to do is stick to our guns, ensure they are physically and mentally exercised, and we and they will come through it. At least they are not smoking, drinking, or doing drugs!

6.2 *Sibling Rivalry*

Our dogs can live together and be best friends. Sometimes, when they reach puberty, things change. Relationships can alter at any time, but the changes that occur in the dog at this stage can provoke a crisis. In the past this has been put down to dominance – our pets trying to control each other as well as us. You may think dominance must exist in homes where there is more than one dog. The continual struggle for status must be the only explanation for why one dog gives a toy up to another, or why dogs that know each other well, would suddenly fight over a bone; why they inexplicably fall out over sleeping areas, and start to growl and bark at each other on sight. But dominance isn't the reason. If you think of their close relationships, and the excellent communication skills dogs naturally possess, wouldn't they more likely give up a toy to their companion because their friend really wants it? (Here, you have it if you're so desperate!) Or maybe they give it up because they simply can't be bothered to argue.

I used to have a Doberman called Tosca. She would sing if she wanted a toy one of the other dogs was playing with. The singing was quiet to begin with, and steadily increased in volume and pitch, until she reached almost operatic heights with a hint of vibrato. She would not stop until she had gained what she wanted. All my dogs learned to give the toy up immediately the quiet singing began, to avoid the racket.

A young pup may suddenly develop the courage or teenage attitude to demand to sleep by the fire. The house's older dog may be irritated because this is the best place during the winter. He won't be happy about giving it up –

but on the other hand, he may know of an even better area, and just glare at the adolescent to get his point across before beetling off to his new hideout.

If all your pets have different likes and dislikes, that helps domestic harmony. For instance, a German shepherd who considered the top of the stairs to be the best position could lie there happily watching the Jack Russell floundering at the bottom. The Jack Russell could be working at his bone below, convinced that his was the better place and occupation – hence no conflict.

6.3 *The Big Juicy Bone Syndrome*

Problems can arise if both dogs want 'the reward' as much as each other and at the same time. How often have you heard someone say 'never have two dogs from the same litter as they fight'? Sibling rivalry is as common in the dog world as it is in the human. If you get two animals that are very similar in personality you are bound to get conflict. In many houses with more than one dog there are items that just cannot be left around, such as pigs' ears or juicy bones, as they cause squabbles. It's a bit like children fighting over the Playstation. Removing the valued items, and replacing them with toys or chews of a lesser value can quickly resolve these issues. However, when all the dogs see the owner as the 'big juicy bone', this can cause major upsets. Squabbling over the owner's attention can lead to awkward situations.

Winnie, a young rescue dog, lived with her family and an older bitch called Sasha. Sasha was Mum's dog and Winnie was supposed to be Dad's, but she never quite cottoned on to this. Dad was not a dedicated dog person and it was Mum who really wanted another dog, utilising the age old 'I've got you a present' scam. As the weeks progressed Winnie became more and more attached to Mum, and began to push Sasha out of the way for attention. Their fights began slowly, with little grumbles between the bitches, always around Mum. But one day Mum came home from work and as she walked through the front door Winnie attacked Sasha, rolling her around the hallway with her teeth firmly embedded in Sasha's neck.

The fight had to be broken up physically, with Mum pulling Winnie forcibly from Sasha, causing deep cuts in Sasha's skin that required stitches. The trigger for such fights was always Mum coming home from work. She tried coming in a different door, keeping the dogs separated when she was out, and only letting them come together once she had been home for a while. None of these strategies worked, as each time the bitches met after Mum had been out for a while, Winnie attacked Sasha. As an experienced dog owner she was reluctant to ask for professional help, and the vet who was doing all the stitching finally called me in. Mum told me she knew what the problem was. Winnie was trying to be top dog over Sasha. Yet she wasn't sure which of the dogs was top, as Winnie gave her toys to Sasha, never tucked into her food until Sasha had finished, and when they played rough and tumble they both spent time on top, pinning the other down. If all the clues led to Sasha being 'Head Honcho', why did Winnie attack her? Mum had already made some changes of her own which revolved around feeding Sasha first, giving her treats and toys first, and most importantly paying her attention first.

Looking at this problem with only status or rank in mind is a mistake. The bitches basically had a strong relationship – they played well, curled up together to sleep, and pined when the other was at the vet's. Sasha simply valued food and toys more than Winnie, who did not want them enough to challenge Sasha. Winnie's big juicy bone was Mum: she was Winnie's most prized possession and getting her attention first, and more importantly holding on to her when she'd been absent, was paramount. Out of the changes Mum had made, only one had an impact, and that was giving Sasha more attention and giving it to her first – simply ensuring that Winnie had to continue competing aggressively for her 'big juicy bone'.

Understanding that rank is not the issue, but reward is, goes a long way to resolving problems like this. Emotionally Winnie could not cope with sharing Mum at that particular moment: she needed her to herself for just a few seconds, and her frustration at the prospect of Sasha taking her 'big juicy bone' was just too much. When they realised the underlying causes of the problem, Mum and Dad could easily see a way through. Dad took over the reins with Sasha, taking her to the office with him, feeding and walking her. This reduced the bond between Mum and Sasha enough to take the pressure off Winnie, and Winnie retained her 'big juicy bone' without bloodshed. This just goes to prove how dogs often compete *for*, not against, their owners!!

6.4 Dog's Do Want to Please – And They Are Selfish!

The majority of dogs find our attention extremely rewarding, and some even find being told off good enough. The desire to please, coupled with the natural need to look up to a parental-type figure, means that a dog can be extremely biddable if given the correct signals, and a communication system he can understand. If communication and signalling is poor between us, the dog will often grab whatever reward they can. This isn't being selfish, it's being a dog!

Teaching a dog to earn all privileges and treats on a quid pro quo basis can help: you scratch my back, and I'll scratch yours! Use a simple task, such as sit or shake paw, which has to be completed before anything the dog values is given to him – such as a treat, a stroke or cuddle, or having his lead clipped on. This can reduce the selfishness to more acceptable levels.

6.5 *Hormone Issues*

There is much controversy surrounding the neutering of dogs – it is an important decision, as once done it cannot be reversed. Seasons in a female can be difficult to manage, as there are strong hormonal changes at these times, which can make the bitch behave differently. There is also the unwanted attention the bitch receives from other dogs, as she unwittingly acts as a beacon signalling to all the males in the area. Hygiene can also be an issue, as some females are not very good at cleaning up their discharges (for which there is now sanitary wear available!). False pregnancies are also a consideration, and can be very real to a female, as I found out.

6.6 *False Pregnancies*

Tosca, my Doberman, had a very strange anatomy. She was born with only half a diaphragm and rib cage and her liver wrapped around her heart. Her chest cavity had abdominal fluid in it, and her heart was enlarged. Tosca's veterinary surgeon was reluctant to neuter her due to her condition. There was no telling whether her female organs would be in the right place, so it could be a case of 'hunt the uterus.'

Tosca had a season, which developed into a false pregnancy. She adopted a little green man (LGM), one of my son's toys, and nurtured it as though it was a real puppy. Taking up residence in my recliner chair, she pushed the 'LGM' to her teats, which were expressing milk, and then licked it afterwards, presumably stimulating it to toilet! Tosca nudged the 'LGM' to make it move. She also became grumpy if we had visitors, or if the children took any notice of the 'LGM' – I was the only one allowed to share her 'baby.'

Tosca's best friend, Mutley, walked around with a confused expression, as his playmate would not leave the chair and sniped at him aggressively if he walked past. About a week after the 'birth', we had visitors and Tosca became very disturbed. What she needed was space, so I took the 'LGM' from her, threw it up the stairs, and sent her up after it to go and get into my bed. For two weeks Tosca hardly ate or drank, and only left her 'baby' for brief periods, in my care, to go to the toilet. But the day her phantom pregnancy finished, she chewed up the 'LGM' and I got my chair back!

This false pregnancy was distressing for Tosca and disruptive for us, so we decided to have her neutered to ensure it never happened again. Once females have had a phantom, they are likely to have another after each season. To deal with a phantom pregnancy without causing undue distress you need to go with the flow – act as though it is a real situation, and the bitch will come out without emotional scars. Taking the 'pup' away and forcing the mother to behave normally, like going out for walks, only increases her distress, and this can leave residual problems to deal with once her hormones are back to normal.

6.7 Does Being a Mother Make a Bitch Nicer?

Some people maintain that allowing a female to have a litter of puppies before neutering her gives her a sweeter nature. I would argue that time and maturity help a dog to develop into a loving, relaxed pet. Waiting until their second or third season to have a litter, and going through the pregnancy and nurturing stage, the bitch would naturally be older and more settled. But I don't think that mating females to make them 'nicer' is a good enough reason for breeding puppies. Being neutered between six months and one year makes very little difference to a female, and it can take away hormonal imbalances such as those that cause false pregnancies. There are downsides to neutering bitches. One is the tendency to put on more weight, and this can be countered by reducing their food intake slightly after the operation. Another, slightly more serious but much less common possibility, is urinary incontinence. This is where the bladder leaks and can be identified by a wet bed in the morning and the general smell of pee around the dog. This requires veterinary treatment – typically drops that are put into the food several times per day to tighten up the bladder (see 7.7).

6.8 The Castration Question

The males amongst us will now wince and cringe and cross their legs as we deliberate the pros and cons of castration. Young male dogs get a huge surge of testosterone at puberty. This can make them a little difficult – though they do get over it. The young bucks can be obstinate, bolshie, belligerent, stroppy, and confrontational. Testosterone gives you bravado and makes you competitive. It makes you do things you would not normally do – you only have to survey the local pubs on a Friday night to see its effects in action!

For a naturally bold and competitive dog, increased testosterone can cause problems, while reducing it a little can be a good thing. On the other hand, a nervous or shy type might benefit from having a little more bravado for a while. For example, if a dog was aggressive to other dogs because it was unsure or afraid of them (which is the major cause of this problem), neutering might make this aggression worse. Making the dog less courageous can increase the amount of fear he feels and then make him more aggressive because he is even more scared. It is as well to think long and hard about neutering a dog at a young age to solve behaviour problems like aggression. You may be very disappointed with the result – and once chopped off, you can't stick them back on! It is a good thing to do if the dog is lifting his leg a lot – particularly if it's indoors – or humping all and sundry. In the long term dogs tend to be healthier if neutered.

It can take up to six weeks to see any real benefit from castration, by which time behaviour patterns can be set and the dog might be reacting to situations through habit. Some say it can take up to six months for a dog to profit from this operation, but that could also be attributed to the dog growing up. Testosterone levels do not stay high for long – they naturally sort themselves out as the dog matures. Of course there are, as with the female, good health reasons for castration. It reduces prostate problems and removes the risk of testicular cancer, amongst other things. But if the dog lacks natural confidence, you could delay castration until he has matured. If, by contrast, your dog is obsessively mounting everything with or without a pulse, castration is your best option.

A few years ago, I went to see an elderly lady who was having problems walking her Golden Retriever, Remus. It was her husband's dog, and he had sadly passed away. Remus was a handful, and the only way she was going to be able to walk him without risk of injury, was by using a head collar. I fitted one, and we went out into the street so I could show her how it worked. The warm sunshine seemed to have an aphrodisiac effect on Remus, as no sooner had we hit the pavement, than he mounted me. His vice-like grip, and pummelling hip action, coupled with his owner laughing hysterically, left me violated and without help. It took the builder from next door to prise the dog off me, but not before I had been paraded in front of the neighbourhood, who had come out to see what the fuss was about. It was hysterical!

If your dog is humping everything there really is no other course of action but to cut his goolies off!!

6.9 *Booster Vaccinations, Worming and Flea Control*

Once our dogs are six months old, they should be wormed regularly regardless of their habits. Dogs don't have to pick up things on walks to become infested. They can get worms from stepping on worm eggs, which become attached to their feet. (Some worm eggs can stay live for up to a year in the earth). Natural cleaning and grooming transfers the eggs to the dog's mouth, and hey presto! Your dog becomes infested. Most dogs will have worms at some time in their lives and it really makes no difference how hygienic you are at home. The same can be said for fleas. A flea can be picked up anywhere. Regular flea treatment is the only sure way to avoid an infestation. Sometimes our dogs share more than just their affections with us!

At around fifteen months of age your dog will require his booster inoculation, to keep him protected against common diseases (see section 2.5). There is some controversy over how often our dogs require immunisation, but it is so worth it to keep nasty illnesses at bay. Just as we listen to our doctors regarding our health, so we should heed the advice of the veterinary profession.

6.10 *Taking Your Dog for his First Booster*

Dogs are used to going out and about with us, so we don't need to catch them or do anything out of the ordinary – just pop the dog in the car. Take special, irresistible food with you to give him immediately after his jabs: this really does take the nastiness away and the dog leaves the vets feeling happy (or happier).

Staying calm and confident helps your dog. Being nervous and stressed makes them worried. Never forget your dog can read you like a book. If your dog is afraid, try not to acknowledge it. When you walk into the consulting room, hand over your vaccination papers. This frees up your hands so you can concentrate on your dog. If he is small, pick him up and pop him on the table. If he is a large dog – don't even try. A vet that wants a large dog on a consulting room table can pick it up himself!

If you and your friends have checked him over regularly, your dog should take his routine examination in his stride. But to help him along, hold a big handful of goodies in front of his nose and slowly release them as he is being examined. When the needle is going in, don't tense up. Stay relaxed and chat to the dog or the vet while maintaining a firm hold of your dog's head in something between a grip and a cuddle. Immediately the vet pulls the needle away, give the dog the rest of the sweeties and carry on chatting. Keeping light-hearted about the event reduces the dog's worries. It is a fact that most dogs wag their tails when their owners laugh or appear happy – use this to your advantage in potentially stressful situations. Forming a relationship with your vet is just like going to the same doctor. It's better if patient and vet know and trust one another.

If your dog becomes aggressive at the vet's, you may need to take special precautions such as muzzling before he goes in. Don't wait until he's had a pop and every one is upset. Muzzle him beforehand, take him in (on a head collar to give you more control even with a small dog) and hold him firmly. Remove the muzzle once he is back outside. If you use a Baskerville muzzle then he can still be treated to something nice straight after. Make sure the muzzle is properly fitted and the dog can't take it off!!!!

6.11 Attention-Seeking

Chasing and 'rugby tackling' our dogs may relieve our frustrations, but it's often the reason they continue to steal our possessions. If they take their own toys and play with them, they may raise a feew 'oohs' and 'aaahs' from the audience, but nicking the mobile phone or TV remote gets a massive and immediate response which includes audience participation in the game – much more fun. This is where we have to be the grown-ups – difficult though it may be.

Ignore the errant dog completely, and instead of reacting, ring the front door bell, bang on a window, walk out of the room and go foraging in the fridge, flick a toy across the room playing catch with another human, or kick a ball around the garden. This distracts the dog away from what he has stolen without giving him any attention. As soon as we focus on him, he has got what he wants. If we shout at him or get involved in his antics by chasing him around the house, we are only teaching him that mischief pays off.

You can use your 'leave it' signal, but he may see this as an opportunity to fleece you of treats. If he steals something again straight away after, then ignore him and follow the suggestions above. The classic sign that he is attention-seeking is stealing, then furtively glancing at you to see if you have noticed. He may even be brazen enough to parade himself in front of you complete with his booty.

Obviously the dog is bored. He needs something more constructive to do. Having ignored him and created a diversion to retrieve the loot it might be an idea to have a short training session or a game of something. Maybe a chew, walk or treat toy. *You need a few minutes to elapse before you start though, or he will connect stealing with getting lots of rewards.*

Attention-seeking comes in many different forms: stealing, barking, whining, whingeing, heavy sighs, scratching the carpet, scratching generally (including scratching themselves), licking things or themselves, pawing, nudging. How often have you had a drink spilt on you by your dog demanding some fuss by nudging your elbow? To give in to some of these demands is not a bad thing – after all we love them and if they need us, why not? *But if the method used to get our attention is particularly annoying and we give in, then our dogs' feeling of success will make them do it again and again.*

6.12 Re-Landscaping the Garden

Some dogs like to dig. They may be digging up a plant, trying to bury a toy or a bone, or doing it just for fun. You think he is out in the garden sunning himself when you catch sight of soil flying past the window and you just know the next Channel Tunnel is underway. I remember being on the telephone one day, minding my own business and nattering to a friend. Suddenly there was a great rustling and my lavender bush entered the living room, propelled by my German shepherd puppy. She dumped it triumphantly at my feet, mud and all. Another of my dogs likes to bury his toys and will spend hours in my office looking for a suitable place – the filing cabinet, my handbag, or under the computer table. If given the opportunity he will extend the search for the perfect hidey-hole into the garden.

There are three ways to deal with digging. We can allow it, under certain restrictions. We can ignore it, as most dogs grow out of this very quickly and making a fuss over it can prolong the activity (this is what I would do and is a must for the laid- back owner). Or we can try and stop it altogether.

Give your dog free access to an area (maybe even a sand pit) so he can dig. The rest of the garden should be fenced off, so he can burrow without hurting your prized flowers. To stop a dog digging huge craters you have to be vigilant. As with all enjoyable but damaging pastimes, you have to make sure you stop it each and every time he tries it. If the word 'No', is not helping, then consider a time-out that is indoors, bringing him into the house and shutting him in the kitchen for two or three minutes (see 4.18). Another suggestion could be utilising a well-aimed hose pipe sprayed in the direction of the dog as soon as his front paws start to 'shuffle'. This can be very effective but may become a game if the dog likes water.

Incidentally, not all dogs dig. Of those that do, most of them will stop within a few days as it becomes boring. There are a few that dig a lot when they're young, but this usually slows down or stops completely as they mature.

6.13 Eating Plants

Some dogs can enjoy an occasional nibble at a plant, either indoors or in the garden. Some plants are poisonous to canines and can make them very poorly. It is as well to know which of your plants is toxic, and keep them out of his reach. The odd chomp on a plant can go unnoticed, but repeated gnawing can damage plants or even kill them. If you can't move the plant out of reach, then ensure the puppy has no access to it unless you are present – deployment of stair gates is useful here. If he tries to eat the plant in your presence then a time- out would be a good idea.

6.14 Dogs Escaping from the Garden

Getting out of the garden is exhilarating. Not only is there the rush of being free, there are neighbours' bins to raid, ponds to play in, cats to chase. When a dog has done this once, he will, almost without exception, try again. He has to be kept in, which means finding the hole in the fence, or the one dug under it, and fixing it. Wire mesh fences should be pegged down at the bottom. If the dog is jumping over the fence, raise the height by adding a trellis to the top. Persistent high-jumpers may need to be kept on a long chain staked in the ground, but you should supervise the dog so he doesn't strangle himself with it. (Use a chain in preference to a rope as a determined dog will chew through a rope in seconds). To avoid garden gates being left open, spring-load them so they swing shut quickly on their own.

The best way of avoiding this problem in the first place is to make your garden escape-proof before you get your dog so he doesn't get a taste of freedom.

6.15 Dogs Rushing at the Front Door

The doorbell is a common trigger for a dog to become over-excited. During puberty, many dogs learn to bark if there is anyone near the house, particularly if they hear a knock at the door. This is totally normal and part of a dog's make-up and development. If the dog knows the person on the other side of the door he may stop, sniff, and put his head on one side. If he doesn't know them he will often become increasingly excited. A dog in a high state of exhilaration can be a bit unpredictable. They may just greet the person with a huge tail and body wag, or they may start jumping up and grabbing at clothes just because they are hyper and out of control. The visitor may not like dogs, or be frightened of them. Just opening the front door could cause that person to run down the drive – and of course the dog will chase a moving target.

If a dog is mildly excited at the front door, we can use a simple 'sit!' to calm them down before opening the door. Others may need to be taught to go outside, or into another room for a few minutes while we get our visitor in and settled. This can easily be achieved by throwing a favourite toy or treat into the other room and closing the door or baby gate behind them. Dogs learn quickly that the doorbell often means they bark, then go into the kitchen and wait to be let out. When we do let the dog through, it is often calmer as it has had a few minutes to settle before it greets the guest.

If he is very persistent and won't be herded elsewhere,

try keeping a lead by the door. Grasp the collar and quickly clip the lead on. We can then use the lead to control the dog (see 5.11).

It can be useful to train your dog in this scenario by getting a friend round to knock on the door. It may take a few attempts for you and your dog to get things right, but it's worth persevering if you don't want your dog going mad when a chance caller knocks on the door.

6.16 Poo Eating (Coprophagia)

This is a particularly unpleasant habit that dogs sometimes adopt. I don't know what is worse, eating their own or someone else's! It can be learned in the litter as puppies copy their mother, or perhaps they eat it just because it's there. Cat poo appears to be a particular delicacy with many dogs. Covered litter trays with tunnel entrances can stop the foraging dog. Dogs are also partial to other animals' poo such as horse, cow and rabbit. They eat poo because they want to and they like it, not because they have something wrong with them or have a dietary deficiency – unless they are not getting fed at all!

If your dog is eating his own poo then firstly, try changing his diet to a high quality super-premium dry food or raw food. This works wonders as these diets are highly digestible and the poo is small, firm and doesn't smell much. They do cost a bit more but usually you have to feed less and if it stops your dog having poo breath then it's *all good*. He should be healthier too. This sorts most cases of coprophagia pretty instantly.

If this doesn't work try clearing it up straight away so that he can't get at it (although the obsessed will whip their heads round and start eating immediately, beating you to it). Another approach is to put a chunk of pineapple in their dinner, or a special preparation (from a pet shop), which makes the poo taste disgusting. If he is eating other animals' poo and you find this unpleasant, then walk him on-lead in those areas while you train him to 'leave it', (see 5.12).

6.17 Boarding Your Pet

There will come a time, such as a family holiday or when you move house, when you need to put your dog into a boarding kennels. This can be traumatic, but usually only for us. We feel guilty about leaving him, and worry about him all the time we are away, only to come back and find he has been absolutely fine and has not pined for us at all. As with kids, it is often a case of 'out of sight, out of mind'. What is cruel is leaving a dog at home with a neighbour popping in to feed it. Dogs require company, exercise, and stimulation and can go 'stir crazy' if left isolated for twenty-three hours per day.

6.18 Introducing Your Dog to Kennels

Taking some of the dog's toys and bedding to his holiday home can help to settle him quickly. Likewise taking his food or organising for him to be fed the same as at home can avoid stomach upsets. A short preliminary visit (maybe over a weekend) can help you and your dog. You'll see how he copes, which will give you some peace of mind when you leave him next time. Your dog learns about his temporary new environment and the most important lesson – you *are* coming back. Leaving quickly, without long emotional farewells, helps him to cope at the point when you walk away (see 3.19).

6.19 Finding a Decent Boarding Kennels

What we as owners require from a boarding kennels can be very individual. As with most things, following a friend's recommendation is possibly the best way of getting the right place for you. Visiting the place, without an appointment, can give you an idea of general cleanliness and hygiene, and you can meet the people who will be caring for your pet. Ask direct questions regarding feeding, cleaning, exercise, insurance, and veterinary support. If your dog is on medication then you need to enquire whether they would be happy to give this.

Check that the kennels has a suitable facility for your dog to be exercised properly – an enclosed pen for off-lead play or a safe on-lead route away from traffic. The housing area should be of a suitable size for your dog to have a sleeping and eating area, *and* a separate place to toilet. Heating in the winter is important for dogs that are used to living in a centrally heated home. Water bowls should be clean and free of any algae with clear fresh water inside.

6.20 Car Travel

It's very important to get your dog used to going in the car. Driving him once a year to the vet can make this particular trip more stressful than it needs to be. The car is, after all, is a very scary place for the novice traveller. It is enclosed, moves, and has a continually changing picture through the window. Dogs used to car travel often go to sleep with the movement and those that become stressed or over-excited in the car can do many annoying or upsetting things. A dog that continually barks, whines and paces in the car is very distracting to the driver. It is also a very difficult problem to solve for the same reason i.e. you still have to drive the car. Prevention is paramount.

Take the dog in the car for short trips, every day if possible. This is something you can start as soon as your puppy arrives home – you don't have to wait for his injections: the earlier, the better. Avoid going somewhere exciting every time, like the park, as this could make car travel a prelude to something exhilarating and increase the likelihood of whining or barking through anticipation. Around the block is good enough if that's all you have time for. Use a travel crate, travel harness, or properly secured dog guard. This is as much for your safety as your dog's. Dogs can do silly things like try and jump on your knee while you are driving. They can also crash into us, or go through the windscreen in an accident. Having a dog sitting on a passenger's knee, without being properly strapped in, invites serious consequences.

Remember that cars are like greenhouses. They become very hot inside in direct sunshine, even when the weather is relatively cool outside. Our dogs do not cope with the heat as well as we do and can quickly become distressed. Their cooling system is not as effective as ours. Dogs do die in hot cars. They also can become so poorly that the effects last a lifetime (such as organ damage). Becoming afraid of the car if they have had an excessive 'heat' experience is also a distinct possibility.

6.21 Coming in from the Garden

Dogs can be a little stubborn about coming indoors when they are busy hunting hedgehogs or digging their way to Australia. Nevertheless, we seem to expect dogs to do our bidding, immediately and without question, and often for no reward. If they're doing something they enjoy, the selfish dog will say no – often by pretending to be deaf. Going outside to physically fetch the dog begins a fantastic game of chase – rewarding the dog hugely for ignoring us in the first place. Coaxing the dog to the back door with a piece of cheese and then grabbing it or telling it off teaches them you are unreliable and not to be trusted.

As with coming when called, there needs to be sufficient motivation in the beginning for a dog to respond (see 4.12, 4.13 and 5.8). Rattling the treat tin or rustling a packet while calling him indicates he is being called in for something he wants. Once the dog is inside, (however long it takes), give him the special treat. Then let him out again. Call the dog in again after ten minutes or so and repeat the treating exercise. The time between calling the dog, and him coming, should get shorter and shorter. Once the dog is responding quickly, reward him occasionally with something extra special like garlic sausage.

6.22 Dog Doors

A dog door is the same as a cat flap – only bigger. It allows the dog access to the garden all the time, which is a good thing in a busy household where the dog's frantic attempts to get your attention to be let out may go unnoticed, or the dog is left alone for many hours. The dog door may require locking at night so he doesn't shoot through it at three in the morning, barking loudly after a local cat. The dog may bark in the garden during the day – reacting to neighbourhood noises. This can cause complaints with no one there to stop him. He may escape out of the garden and run riot in the local vicinity and be picked up by the dog warden. Security is a factor too. Large dogs require dog doors of a large size – which a person could perhaps crawl through.

You need to think about the consequences before installing a dog door.

CHAPTER SEVEN

From Eighteen Months Onwards and Other Stuff

7.1 Emotional Maturity

With any luck we should see all our hard work paying off as our dogs mature. They become calmer, less demanding, and a real pleasure to be with. This happens slowly at any time from eighteen months onwards. Some mature early, others late, rather like us. Emotional maturity has nothing to do with size, growth rate, or sexual maturity. We are talking about our puppy going from a child to a teenager and on to a fully mature adult.

They play less, they sleep longer, and they can appear quite contented for most of the time. They understand and are part of our household routine, and cope well with daily life. We've also come to know them, and they know us. We understand what situations they can and can't cope with – though it's easy to forget, as they become less demanding, that they still need to be played with, exercised, and kept occupied with little bursts of pleasure throughout the day. Like us, they still need fun in their lives!

7.2 Bringing a Baby into the House

Having a baby was the biggest thing of my life. It turned everything upside down – and still does! I never believed I could love anything more than my dog. When Lauren was born I had Hannah, my German shepherd, and she was three years old. Hannah had never been up close to a baby or young child before. Coming home from the hospital, I knew Hannah would be ecstatic to see me, so I left Lauren in the car with my husband and went in alone. She bounced about everywhere. I remember standing there looking at her and thinking, 'She is SO big'. Feeling protective about a baby is totally normal, but I never suspected that Hannah would make me worry about Lauren. Taking a deep breath I went out to the car and fetched Lauren. Sitting down on the settee with her, I invited Hannah up for a cuddle beside me. She sniffed at Lauren, and poked her with her nose – and Lauren was accepted. She was even more acceptable when Hannah discovered the delights of baby puke and tasty nappies!!

I changed nothing at home. Hannah was still allowed to sleep upstairs, get on the sofa, and do all the things she normally did. I didn't fuss about Hannah's hygiene. She liked to lick Lauren, but she was a healthy dog who was regularly wormed. I believe you can be too clean around kids, which does nothing for their immune systems. I grew up with Puffin, a Boston terrier who was always licking me and wouldn't leave my side. My Mum bought a playpen to keep me and Puffin apart, but when she left the room for a few minutes, Puffin got into the pen with me! Of course you don't want a dog licking a baby all day, but a couple of gentle 'kisses' won't hurt.

The only problem I encountered was when Lauren started to stand. Like most German shepherds, Hannah was an exceptional housedog, who charged and barked at the front door if anyone knocked. Lauren was in her baby bouncer one day (a contraption that hangs off a door frame that babies can bounce and turn in), when someone knocked. Hannah sped to the door as usual, brushing passed Lauren on her way and sending her into a fast spin. Lauren thought this was great and giggled all the way, but we never used the device on that door again. When she was walking, Lauren quickly learned to lean out of the way to let Hannah pass if the door knocker went.

Safety is the biggest concern when a baby is brought into the home and the dog is only one aspect of it.

Where children and dogs are concerned, we always have to be one step ahead. The introduction of a baby into the home should be a good thing. Panicking over what the dog might do doesn't help anyone. Thinking clearly and logically about potential mishaps (something you get into the habit of with children anyway), as well as careful supervision, should ensure that the dog and child are safe in each other's company. Obvious things to avoid are leaving a baby unattended on the floor with a dog – which might tread on the child if something exciting suddenly happens. Some dogs are fond of curling up in warm and comfortable spots – cradles, cots, and prams are just the sort of place a terrier might be attracted to for instance. If a baby was in there acting as a hot water bottle, he may lie on top – potentially very dangerous. Using a cat net to stop the dog getting in, closing the door to keep him out or putting a baby gate across the threshold – is a sensible precaution.

Babies do not bother most dogs. It is when they start crawling and investigating their surroundings that he might become frightened or worried. From the dog's point of view, this little pink bundle has sat (wriggling and squawking) in a bouncer chair or something similar for months. Suddenly it can move, and heads towards the dog, giggling and gurgling all the way. If the dog has been kept away from the baby, this sudden mobility can be shocking. The dog that has been around the baby from the beginning often takes the new development in its stride.

Now the baby is investigating everything – including the dog! It might stick its fingers in nose holes, or pull hair. Most dogs are very tolerant of this, but we must remember that everyone has a boiling point. If the baby is hurting the dog, and it cannot escape, it will defend itself – eventually. Giving the dog time and space away from the baby, and not letting the baby maul it, prevents unpleasant situations.

If you are concerned about animal hygiene and your baby, or about the two interacting in areas where your dog is allowed to come and go, you should make the necessary changes in the months before your baby arrives. A sudden alteration to the dog's lifestyle (like shutting them out of the family area), coupled with you devoting most of your time and energy to the new baby, can make your dog feel unloved, anxious, and insecure. Teaching your dog beforehand not to jump up (see 5.11), and how to entertain itself (see 4.22 to 4.27), can make all the difference. Once the baby is in (and ruling the roost), a relationship will develop with the dog over the months and years – one the child will never forget.

It can be difficult to bite the bullet and let a big bouncy dog meet a new baby. Pumpkin, a young bouncy Labrador, was shut into the utility room when the baby arrived. Walks dwindled to nothing as the baby was difficult to settle, and Mum was unable to walk the dog and push the pram because Pumpkin pulled on the lead. Mum and Dad were worried that she would hurt the baby because when she was let in, she bounded about the living room, threw her toys around, and jumped up at the cradle. Pumpkin was just over-excited at finally being allowed back into the family area, but then she was sent back to the utility room before she had a chance to settle. Because she was upset at the sudden changes, and had nothing better to do, Pumpkin ate the utility room.

Her destructive behaviour stopped when Pumpkin was given a variety of toys and other things to amuse her (see 4.22 and 4.27). Fitting a head collar stopped her pulling and allowed Mum to take her around the town with the baby in the pram or sling. This device was also used to bring Pumpkin into the living room when the baby was present. When the baby was in the nursery sleeping, Pumpkin was given free access to the living room to reduce the novelty factor. Once Pumpkin was given back the freedom of the house, she calmed down and took baby events in her stride. She quickly learned that the baby was a source of pleasure and took great delight in cleaning up spilled baby food – especially the floor around the high chair!

7.3 Moving House

This can be an exceptionally stressful time for all concerned and when we are stressed, our dogs can become worried. They know something is going on, but they don't understand what! If his behaviour changes slightly at this time – this is the reason why.

At the packing stage dogs can become very unsettled. The environment is changing by the hour from the normal home to cardboard city. When I moved several years ago, I put my dog into kennels on the day of the move. We moved into our new home, unpacked most things, and then I fetched her home. Hannah showed no signs of concern and readily accepted the change.

7.4 Fun Activities

When your dog is fully grown, you may take up Agility or Flyball with him. Agility involves jumping through hoops, climbing over large obstacles, running through tunnels and hurdling. Flyball has four jumps that the dog has to hurdle at speed, which leads to a box-like device that the dog has to activate with its paw. When activated the box shoots a ball into the air that the dog then catches and takes back over the four jumps. These are quite energetic sports and can put pressure on a developing dog's skeleton – which is why it is not advisable to start them too young. There are two different types of agility / flyball venues – those that do it for fun and those that encourage competition.

A weekly swimming trip to a local doggy hydropool can work wonders for a dog's fitness, and most of them love it. Swimming is great exercise at any age, and playing fetch in a pool for most dogs is a wonderful experience. Sadly, swimming in local rivers and lakes is not recommended, as your dog is likely to contract all sorts of infections.

7.5 Getting Over Operations

Thanks to recent breakthroughs in veterinary medicine it is now possible to operate on many disabling conditions. But for dogs that have undergone major surgery, the recuperation period can be long and painful. Try giving them some kind of stimulus that will cheer them up without causing further injury or discomfort. After all, suffering pain without gain can lead to depression, which can debilitate an animal to the point when it needs professional help.

Ellie, a Springer Spaniel, had a hip-replacement operation when she was about two years old. She had to be kept in a crate at home for many weeks. There were other dogs in the house that she might have played with, if she'd been allowed to roam free. On-lead exercise gave her little pleasure. Springer spaniels like to run off-lead, sniffing and flushing things out of bushes. Ellie became moody, frustrated, and grumpy, and started snapping at her owner and her canine companions. I suggested feeding her each meal differently, using a combination of food-dispensing toys, food-scattering, and getting Ellie to earn some of her dinner by giving a paw, sitting and lying down when asked (see 4.21 to 4.25). This was done not at set times, but throughout the day, so Ellie had regular bursts of pleasure. It was enough to keep her sane, and her recovery was accelerated through physiotherapy and swimming in a hydropool. This helped to rebuild her muscles so she could get back to normal exercise and play.

Dogs recovering from surgery are often prescribed weeks of kennel rest, which can be stressful to owner and dog. Swimming is non-weight bearing exercise and is unlikely to interfere with recovery. By improving fitness and increasing cardiovascular strength, post-operative surgery recovery times can be greatly reduced.

My own dog, Bigun, went through a hip replacement in 2005 and the physiotherapy / hydrotherapy reduced his recovery time by many weeks.

7.6 When Your Dog is Poorly

Like us, our dogs' behaviour can be affected when they are unwell. They can lose interest in life and become sullen, grumpy, or very clingy. Getting them well again is a physical as well as an emotional priority. A sudden change in your dog's behaviour usually indicates there is something physically wrong. If your normally happy-go-lucky canine suddenly turns clingy and morose, if it starts to toilet in the house when it has never done this before, or if it lies in its bed growling at everyone – take it to the vet before you consult a behaviour specialist!

Some friends once called me to say their dog had just bitten their ten-year-old child. Popping round to see them, I found Sparky the dog hiding under the dining room table while the family had gathered in the living room. They said Sparky had been acting weird all day, and he wouldn't come out from under the table. The child had gone into the dining room to try and coax him out, and Sparky had bitten him on the hand. Sparky was normally a very social dog, that loved to play and adored visitors, but I could get no reaction from a very sad-looking pooch. The vet was called and discovered Sparky had a severe tummy problem, which was causing him great pain. He was taken into the surgery and treated, and never bit anyone again.

For more details on giving tablets and medication see 2.8 to 2.11.

7.7 Incontinence

This can be very distressing for old dogs that have been clean in the house all their lives. Getting cross or exasperated at having to mop up after them all the time, can make the distress worse. Getting the geriatric to sleep on incontinence pads in their favourite areas reduces the mess they make. Cleaning the soiled coat and skin stops them from becoming sore. At this stage in the animal's life, when the vet can't do much to help, we have to try and keep them as happy and comfortable as we can.

Females can suffer from urinary incontinence, sometimes as a result of neutering. This can be misread as a house-training problem. The difference is that they do not know they are doing it because the pee seeps out very slowly. You commonly find soiled bedding or carpet where the dog has slept. They often smell of urine, as they do not feel the pee coming out, especially when asleep. Being told off can be very confusing, as they have no idea why you are cross. This is a medical problem that has a very easy solution. A trip to the vet can settle this condition quickly.

For naturally hygienic animals, soiling in the home through incontinence can cause anxiety and stress. This will be greatly reduced if you clean up quickly (see 3.23), make no reference to the mess, and ensure the dog knows it is loved by giving it a cuddle.

7.8 *Anorexia*

When our dog refuses to eat it, it causes great concern. First find out if the dog is ill. If there is no obvious sickness, we need to look at the food they are being offered. Are we feeding too much? Many dog food manufacturers rather overstate the amount needed and sometimes feeding a smaller amount solves the problem instantly. Changing the diet or flavour of the food can stimulate appetite again, but altering the manner they are fed can *inspire* them to eat again. If your dog will take a piece of food from your hand, but will not eat it out of the bowl, then it is the way the food is presented, not the food itself that is the problem. Using food toys, pieces of their dinner as training treats or scattering the food in the garden or kitchen can get the dog back on track (see 4.21 to 4.25). If a dog won't eat his food, putting it down for ten minutes and then taking it away again is not much encouragement. It's rather like putting spinach in front of a child and telling them they have to eat it. The removal of the spinach after ten minutes is a huge relief!

Keats was a guide dog. He was very good at his job, but not easily motivated by food, and found wading through a large bowl of dry food twice a day quite punishing. Concerned that he might lose his guide dog, his owner tried hand-feeding Keats. The dog wanted to eat to please his owner, but found it too much and became very stressed: he would roll his eyes on seeing his food being prepared, and run out of the room. Changing the way the food was presented, and the type of food he had, worked immediately. Putting him on a performance diet – concentrated food intended for hard-working dogs – allowed us to feed him much less. Placing the food inside toys and throwing bits around the room made eating more of a game than anything. Keats even started eating out of a food bowl again when this was made part of his varied feeding pattern.

Fussing over the dog while it is refusing to eat can make the situation much worse. One of my dogs was three years old when I got him. His teeth were discoloured, and he came with several tins of wet dog food, with the explanation that he wouldn't eat dry stuff of any variety. I only offered him dry food, but he got it in a variety of ways – and his teeth now gleam...

I learned a lesson about fussy feeding when Tosca, my Doberman female, had a false pregnancy. As she wouldn't eat during this time, we offered her tasty titbits on top of her meal to entice her. Her appetite returned when the phantom pregnancy was over, but then she took to sitting and looking at the fridge instead of eating her normal food, waiting for a titbit of ham or cheese to magically appear. Once I got wise to this, I let her get hungry, and she began to eat normally again, like the piglet she always was.

Dogs are very clever. They will hold out for something special if we teach them that they'll be offered it if when they don't tuck into their food straight away.

7.9 How Long Do Dogs Live?

A dog's lifespan can depend on its breed – in very general terms, the larger the dog, the shorter the life. Jack Russell terriers can live to their mid-teens and remain active and fit all their lives, always ready to chase a squeaky toy. Mastiffs and other giant breeds may only live to seven or eight years of age, and slow down significantly at five or six. Short-necked and stumpy-nosed breeds tend to have a shorter lifespan, irrespective of their size, due to breathing difficulties.

Many breeds of dogs develop mobility problems, and although all sizes are susceptible, the effect is much greater on large dogs because of the weight they carry. Keeping any dog slim (irrespective of breed type) throughout its life can increase the lifespan and they stay healthier and more mobile for longer. Just like us!

7.10 *Mobility Problems*

There are many factors that affect our dogs' ability to move freely. The most common is being overweight. Obesity causes not only extra stress on the muscles, tendons, and joints, but can also create other health issues, as it can in us. If your dog waddles towards you to collect his favourite piece of cheese, try offering raw carrot instead. Most dogs enjoy raw vegetables as much as any other treat. There are no calories, and because they need to be chewed, they can help with dental hygiene as well. Use low-fat dog treats, light dog foods, even low-fat cheese. Every little bit helps. Couple this with *gradually* increasing exercise and reducing meal sizes (or changing to a light version of the food), and your dog can lose weight steadily.

Crash diets are as bad for our dogs as they are for us. Reduce weight slowly by altering the types of foods given and encourage the dog to be more active generally. As with us, they do need edible pleasures in their lives. The most effective diets people go on do not exclude everything, but allow appealing food in moderation. Apply this principle to your dog's diet to avoid him becoming unhappy.

Dietary supplements are a good idea in the older dog, such as products that contain glucosamine and chondroitin. These can help significantly with movement problems caused by arthritis, a painful disease of the joints that our dogs can suffer from at any age. Keeping them mobile and active is important, as the joints can literally start to seize up. Swimming is an excellent way to keep supple and mobile, without putting any undue pressure on bone structure. It is also ideal for rebuilding muscle that is wasted through lameness, especially when a weight-bearing exercise would prove too painful.

Swimming exercises every muscle in the body, but hydrotherapy for dogs needs to take place in warm water. Cold water causes blood vessels to narrow, reducing blood flow to the muscles, so the muscles won't work properly. Remember that water in lakes and rivers is very cold, and that it can also carry diseases.

When they swim regularly in warm water, most arthritic dogs rapidly improve, and are able to climb stairs and walk for longer periods. Dogs that develop tissue abnormalities in their hips and elbows compensate for the pain and discomfort by altering the way they stand and walk. This can make other muscles in the body tense and the dog feels generally worse. Swimming relaxes these muscles and tightens tendons, helping the dog to walk and stand properly. If a dog has suffered severe pain, it can sometimes be frightened of putting weight on that area and carry on limping even though the problem has been resolved. Swimming helps to build the animal's confidence in using its leg or shoulder once more.

While rehabilitation is the main aim of hydrotherapy, one aspect that should never be forgotten is fun. Most dogs love to swim, and even those breeds that are not classed as natural swimmers will usually find enjoyment after a few sessions. Swimming is also great exercise for puppies and young dogs, as their little bodies are not being forced in any way.

7.11 Allergies

Allergic reactions or intolerances are becoming more commonplace with our pets. One of the most common is reactions to flea bites – one flea bite can cause a whole area on the dog to become red, itchy, and so inflamed it requires veterinary treatment. De-fleaing the house and using a strong anti-flea treatment reduces the risk of being bitten, but will not stop the odd bite from a rogue flea. Some natural remedies such as VetIQ Protect-Um® reduce the chance of a fleabite by making the dog unappealing to the flea. For serious fleabite allergies, using the natural approach together with veterinary treatments is a sensible way to manage the problem.

Food intolerances such as reactions to chicken, beef, wheat, and dairy products can cause a range of health problems such as sickness, diarrhoea, or skin problems. These are relatively easy to resolve – *once you know what foods to avoid.* An exclusion diet, followed under veterinary supervision, is one of the ways to work out exactly what product is causing the problem. There are also blood tests available, so it's well worth a trip to the vets.

Some dogs now develop hayfever. Like us, they can be allergic to absolutely anything. I am allergic to metal, shampoo, concrete, and lettuce – where's the sense in that?

7.12 Losing Their Senses

Dogs can be born with deafness or blindness as a disability. They usually manage very well, as they have never known life to be any different. But losing their senses through age or illness can be quite traumatic.

I grew up with a Boston terrier, Puffin, who was almost blind by the time he was five. He coped remarkably well at home and only appeared to have difficulty if we moved the furniture. Taking him out was not easy as he walked into things if we weren't watching him. One day at Charing Cross train station in London, he fell down the gap between the platform and the train. My father was busy talking to the train driver and thought Puffin was just pulling on the lead when in fact he was hanging himself! (Puffin did survive the incident so no tears please

Hearing loss in old dogs is fairly common. Their deafness

causes us very few problems (there may be some increase in barking), and can even be a bonus to dogs that are frightened of thunder and fireworks. Tolerance towards loud noises can reduce as a dog ages and some acquire noise-related phobias in their old age (a bit like granny telling you to turn the stereo down). When she was about eight years old my German shepherd, Hannah, became very scared of the sound of a mobile phone bleeping when the battery was low, and the bangs and rattles the dishwasher made. She had never shown signs of being frightened of noises before, and was a keen spectator of fireworks.

Kipper, a crossbreed, was twelve before he showed fear of anything. Almost overnight he became terrified of thunder, rain, fireworks, and any other sudden loud bangs. His panic was so intense he needed to be on a lead in the house if it began to rain outside, as he would hurt himself in his attempts to escape. No one really knows why older dogs are more susceptible like this. Perhaps as more dogs survive to ripe old ages the more we will understand.

7.13 Losing Their Marbles

Senility can come to us all, including our beloved dogs. They may seem confused and stare vacantly during busy times like family gatherings and Christmas. Old dogs can feel crotchety if their routine is dramatically altered, and there is an increase in noise and movement levels in the house. If they become growly we need to snap them out of this by making them feel better quickly. A simple answer is to move them away from the melee and into a quiet area, giving them something nice to chew on. Getting a younger dog to revitalise the old one can work wonders, as the old old-timer can regain some of its youthfulness with a young playmate. It can also go horribly wrong, with the grumpy old devil refusing to have anything to do with the young upstart, except for being unfriendly and aggressive. You should only ever get another dog because you want one – not to sort out problems with the incumbent.

We do have to take extra care of our geriatric dogs by ensuring they have peace and quiet from the kids and other animals. While our whole lives cannot always revolve directly around them, we should show understanding of their needs at this time in their lives, and try to keep them as settled, comfortable, and happy as possible.

As they get older the nutrition they need changes. Some high quality brands now make special brain foods for the older dog to keep them mentally active and alert. Being a bit of a sceptic, I tried one with Bigun who was then twelve years old. It worked a little too well and he started to behave in ways I had not seen for years. It was a little shocking to see my dog that slept for much of the day suddenly getting into mischief and instigating play – but fabulous at the same time.

CHAPTER EIGHT

Taking on a Rescue Dog

8.1 Choosing Your Rescue Dog

Choose your dog with your head *and* your heart. If you are ninety years old, don't go for a six-month-old German shepherd, even if it is the most handsome beast on the block. Rescuing a dog can be difficult. It may have been through several homes and have a multitude of problems, or it might be a perfectly well balanced animal who won't give you a minute's trouble. You don't really know what he will be like until he's been living with you for several weeks. You perhaps won't even know exactly why the dog is in the shelter to begin with. A dog can behave very differently in a rescue shelter from the way it behaves in a house. They are like a puzzle that you have to piece together over time. A dog that has suffered abuse often needs extra time and a very loving 'parent' in order to build up trust. Seriously traumatised, the dog can find daily life very frightening.

You shouldn't look on a rescue as a cheap way of gaining a dog, as the donation to the shelter could will be just the beginning of your financial commitment. Take a rescue dog into your home because you like that individual, and want it to live with you.

Consideration should be given to size, age, breed, exercise requirements, and how much grooming it the dog is going to need. These are things to think about before going to the shelter, so your heart does not take over. You may have to visit the shelter many times before you find the right dog for you. It is wise to take time over your decision – he could be with you for many years. Take the dog you fancy for a walk around the shelter. Stroke it all over once it is relaxed with you. Ask direct questions about the history, so you know as much as possible about it before you make your choice.

If you have a dog already, take it into the shelter to introduce them. Most centres have an enclosed area for this. If you have a cat at home, ask at the centre whether the dog you like is used to cats. A trip to the cattery with the dog on a lead will give an indication of how it copes, but you need to be aware that it may behave differently off-lead and in a house. You also need to know about any medical conditions the dog has, so you can find out about treatment costs and how much time you might need for nursing. Don't feel bad about saying 'no' or 'maybe' about a dog. It is better to think the choice through properly than to take the dog home, only to return it within a week. This just adds to the dog's list of traumas.

Do you want an adult, a juvenile, or a young pup? Have a long think about your needs as an owner, before you go and lose your heart to the first 'hair ball' you see.

Most rescue centres require your house and garden to be vetted by an inspector. This can be frustrating, as once you have chosen your rescue you naturally want to take them home, but it is ultimately for the safety of the dog.

Most pedigree breeds have a specific rescue charity. If you are looking for a 'second-hand' pedigree pet, one of these associations may be able to help.

Neutering rescue dogs is standard policy for most charities. If the dog is not old enough to be neutered, many places give you a voucher to use at your vet's. Your new rescue should be fully vaccinated and treated for fleas and worms on leaving the sanctuary. The medical paperwork, signed by a veterinary surgeon, should list these vaccinations, the date for the next booster injections, and on-going flea and worming instructions. Many rescue shelters microchip the dogs before they leave.

8.2 A Check-Up at the Vets

Not all dogs receive a medical at rescue shelters. It is advisable to take your rescue to your own veterinary surgeon for a general health check (see sections 2.6 and 6.9). Getting sound professional advice on feeding, weight loss, weight gain, and checking that he has no eye, ear, or skin infections, or general health concerns, is the best way to start. It is also useful to see how he reacts to being handled at a veterinary practice, although this can change once the dog settles into life with you.

Ideally this would be a good time to discuss and take out some health insurance.

8.3 Taking Your Rescue Home

Firstly, you need a car harness, a properly fitted dog-guard, or a travel crate. Loose dogs are hazardous in a car, and you don't yet know how the dog will react to travelling. Use absorbent material to help with any accidents. For further details see sections 3.11, 3.23 and 6.20.

8.4 Introducing to the Family

Ideally, your rescue will have met members of your family at the shelter. This is a big day for him, full of uncertainties. Dogs generally don't like being crowded. If they are in a new place, with new people, they like to take their time and approach things slowly. Rushing up to a dog can make it scared. It is better for everyone to sit back and relax and allow him to come to them, when he is ready. Your rescue dog may have had many unsettling experiences. Taking things slowly with him can help him settle quickly.

Show your new dog the garden first. Wait with him until he has gone to the toilet before allowing him to explore the house. This gets toilet rules underway quickly. Have a sleeping area, basket, or crate prepared for him, and place some treats or a nice toy inside. The water bowl should be in a place he can reach easily and have access to at all times. If you have another dog at home, it is advisable to introduce them at the shelter or in the local park before walking them back home together. This avoids canine confrontations at the front door. For more details see sections 3.14 to 3.17.

8.5 Leaving Your Rescue Dog

The nurturing bond is very important to dogs. Having been in a shelter they may have been deprived of proper parental love. Some dogs have a tendency to over-bond with their new parent, and are literally grief-stricken if left without them. To compensate for their previous unhappiness, most of us tend to be over-attentive to our new dogs. If they are ever to be left alone – and it is unlikely the dog will be with someone for every minute of the day – we must help them by leaving them for very short periods almost immediately. Learning that we go out but always come back is imperative. For more details on leaving your rescue and how to use a crate, see sections 3.19 and 3.20.

8.6 Settling at Night

As with puppies, the first few nights are usually the worst. Having decided where you want your dog to sleep, you need to ensure he is tired. An early evening play session or walk with a dog can help him to 'chill out' later on. Playing a radio at low volume can stop him feeling completely alone and reduce his reaction to strange noises outside. A side-light or glow-light in their sleeping area for the first few nights can help him to settle. Many dogs find being confined behind a closed door worrying, but cope very well with a baby gate that they can see through.

For more details see section 3.18.

8.7 Allow Your New Rescue Time and Space

Your new rescue may make mistakes in the first few days and weeks. He needs to learn about you and your household. Your house rules may be entirely different to what he is used to. Decide where you want him to be allowed to go, and stick to these rules using clear signals. For information see sections 4.9 to 4.18. Re-training is discussed later in this chapter (section 8.11).

Mutley, one of my rescue dogs and quite possibly the best dog I ever owned, did a pee up the kitchen door on his first night of living with us. When I came down in the morning, I greeted them all as usual, and popped them into the garden to toilet. I then cleared up his mess (out of his sight). No reference was made to his mistake. He never did it again. If I had told him off, he would not have known exactly why I was cross, as too long had elapsed between his action and its discovery. Disciplining him could have made him worried or frightened of me. On his first day with us he was so happy running free in the garden (he had been at the shelter for many months), he didn't want to come in at night. Using a nice tasty biscuit I coaxed him in through the door and calmly closed it behind him. Without making a big fuss Mutley was finally indoors and happy about it. It also began teaching him to come when called (see 6.21, 5.8 and 5.9).

Keeping calm and dealing with issues immediately they

crop up teaches our dogs quickly what we want. Shouting and becoming angry at their mistakes can make them mistrust us. They can do no wrong until they know what is right.

8.8 Bonding With Your Rescue Dog

Gaining his confidence and trust should be your primary objective for the first few days. You are both strangers, and it takes time to get to know each other. On average it can take two weeks for a dog to settle into its new home, but some take much longer. Mutley trusted me almost immediately, but found being close to other members of the family, difficult. He would growl and show his teeth in a very defensive way. Those family members Mutley was bothered by had very little to do with him in the first few weeks. They backed off completely from him, and allowed Mutley to get used to them being there without any pressure. Dropping treats into Mutley's bed as they walked past, throwing a ball for him in the garden, and taking him out for a walk after I had clipped on the lead, made them a source of 'goodies' in Mutley's eyes. I feel certain that if anyone had become angry with Mutley when he growled, Mutley would never have felt relaxed around him or her.

Feeding dogs little and often throughout the day can also speed up the bonding process. As a 'parent' you are cultivating the dependent side of the animal's nature. Chatting to your new dog in a light-hearted manner will help him regard you as a source of comfort and pleasure. Taking the time to stroke him and play with his toys will increase his happiness. Giving attention when he asks for it is what good parenting is about – though this depends on how he goes about asking! (For more information on attention seeking, see section 6.11).

8.9 When to Let the Rescue Dog off the Lead

As long as your new dog has had his full vaccination course, you can walk him out straight away. Letting him off the lead is a risk in the beginning, and it's probably better to use an extender lead or long line to see how he reacts to being called. You don't want to be standing there with an empty lead, the dog just a cloud of dust on the horizon. Teaching him right from the start to come when you call him, especially if you've given him a new name, is a must in order to avoid such embarrassment (see sections 5.3, 5.8 and 5.9).

8.10 Re-Training Your Rescue

You may not want your new dog to take over your sofa, your bed, or your recliner chair as and when he wants, even if it is something he is accustomed to. Re-training to get what you want from your dog can be difficult if approached in too firm a manner. Shouting and physically pulling the dog off your chair can make him feel threatened and cause him to growl at you. Dogs sit on the furniture because it is comfortable and they like it because we sit there too. Pushing them off can be quite stressful for them.

Firstly, you need to provide a place that is theirs, and equally comfortable. This could be a nice snuggly duvet-type bed for a dog. The bed should be in the family area, but they also need one where they can have their own quiet time.

The moment you see your dog attempting to get onto the sofa, tell them 'No!' calmly but firmly. Coax him onto the dog bed using something tasty like a Kong® toy, stuffed with goodies, and stroke calmly to encourage him to settle down. Using this method you are telling him firmly what you don't want, while making the alternative very pleasurable. Dogs learn very quickly, as long as you are *consistent* in what you do for several weeks (telling him once or twice won't work). A dog will still attempt to get onto the furniture when you aren't there. You can only stop him by shutting the door to the living room, or by blocking access to the furniture (sticking the hoover on it!).

Toilet training can be a little hit and miss with a dog that has been in a rescue centre, perhaps for many months. Re-training them is exactly the same as teaching a puppy from the beginning (see section 3.22 and 3.23).

A dog may have forgotten his previous training (if he had any), and be a little unruly. Establishing a communication system using clear signals of success and failure can help him learn quickly and minimise confusion between you. (Further details are in sections 4.9 to 4.18 and Chapter Five).

Start these strategies from day one and you will avoid the need for further re-training later.

CHAPTER NINE

Dealing with Death

9.1 *Knowing When to Let Go*

The perfect death is to die peacefully while sleeping. This is probably what we all want for our dogs (and ourselves!). Legalised euthanasia is a controversial issue when it comes to people, with many heartfelt arguments for and against. There can be ulterior motives to do with love or money where people are concerned – it may not be the individual's welfare that is the sole consideration. But when your dog can no longer cope with age or sickness, it can only benefit from being released from its misery. It is pure punishment to see something or someone you love suffering right before your eyes.

They have been our most faithful friends and companions over the years. We have nurtured and cared for them, and they in turn have given us amusement, pleasure, and unquestioning love. Through thick and thin, good times and bad times, we have relied on our dog always greeting us like a long-lost friend. Now we have to make perhaps one of the most difficult decisions of our lives. At what point do we think that our dog's quality of life is so poor that there is no longer any pleasure in it for him? No one can answer this question for you. It is your decision, your choice, your burden.

Being allowed to die with dignity and the minimum of

suffering is the last great gift you can give your friend.

9.2 *The Final Act*

Having made the decision to have your dog put to sleep, discuss the options with your veterinary practice. Many vets will come out to the house, if this causes less distress to your dog. Some dogs do not like going to the vet's, and a final visit there may be something we can avoid. It is also worth considering whether you would like your dog cremated, or if you are going to bury him, and organising this when you book the appointment. It may seem cold-hearted, but you will not feel like talking about these things at the time and they do need to be sorted out. When I had Hannah put to sleep, I pre-paid over the telephone. The last thing you want is to be presented with a bill that you have to pay in a busy reception area. Veterinary practices often offer a private cremation service, which includes an urn and brass plaque.

It is just an injection. It is over with very quickly. We laid Hannah down in my lap on the floor, and I cuddled her as the vet did his bit. She never acknowledged the needle, just looked into my eyes and the light faded. I sat and cuddled her for ages afterwards, saying my last goodbye. When I finally left, it did not feel like a betrayal to leave her there on the floor – she was free of pain and at peace.

9.3 Grieving

Now the grieving process starts. In the first few hours and days we need time to reflect on the life we shared together. We do not necessarily grieve at the manner of their dying, but mourn the fact they are no longer present. The feeling of loss or emptiness can last for a very long time. The house is too quiet. Walks are seemingly pointless. Going home is no longer a pleasure.

Many people scatter the ashes of their dog on favourite walks, or bury them in the garden. Keeping the urn secreted in a private place in the house was my choice (I now have quite a collection in a room we have nicknamed 'The Crypt'). Grief is so personal – we all cope with it differently. When Hannah died, I cleaned. The house and car were polished, scrubbed, and vacuumed. The sight of her hair on the settee and carpet and dog snot on the windows of the car made me look for her, momentarily forgetting she was gone.

It is natural to mourn the death of a dog. They are part of the family and the bond between us is incredibly strong. Having lived with us perhaps for many years, it takes a big adjustment to get used to life without them.

When I collected Hannah's urn several days after, my young daughter was amazed that they had fitted such a large dog into such a small box. She was very impressed. A few days later we attended the funeral of one of my friends. Lauren, my daughter, was very concerned that Hannah might be alone, so I explained to her that Hannah was now in heaven, with my friend. As we drove away from the funeral, my daughter asked, 'Are we leaving Heaven now?' Death, through the eyes of a child…

9.4 The Dog Left Behind

It must be very strange for a dog to watch its life-long friend go out of the front door and never come back, while the whole house is in tears and bursting with emotion. Our dogs feels grief too. They miss their companion and may need extra attention from us to help them cope. We know how bad we feel about our loss. Imagine what it must be like for their buddy who has eaten, slept, and played with them and is now on their own.

It can help, when dogs are very close, to show the surviving one the body of the deceased. This gives them an explanation for their friend's disappearance. We have to ensure our dog doesn't feel depressed by the loss of their mate. Practical things we can do include extra walks and games and being there for them. We can raise their general mood by giving special treats or new toys. If there's anything they likes to do – offer more of it. A dog may be reluctant to eat if it is unhappy – encourage him to eat using food toys or by making food fun (see sections 4.21 to 4.25). Playing little games with the food can increase appetite and make him feel better.

9.5 Getting Another Dog

For some (myself included), this is the only avenue to take. I have lived with dogs my whole life, and my house is not a home without a few beasties floating around. We cannot replace the friend we have lost, but we can make a space in our hearts for a new one. You may think at the time that you could never love another dog the way you did your last, or face the grief that comes when you lose them, but somehow we animal lovers find room for someone else. Another dog may help the one left behind to stop moping about the house. But you must also consider your current situation, and the practicalities of having a new puppy with all they entail. The age of your existing dog may make it prudent to have an older, more mature animal as a companion.

It is not a slight on our recently recently passed pal to go and find another. It is a compliment of the highest order. Life with them was so fulfilling and enjoyable that we are now hooked on dogs forever!

Printed in Great Britain
by Amazon

66230992R00098